Ngā Pūrehu Kapohau

A Literary Homage to
Pātea, Waverley, and Waitōtara

Edited by

Trevor M Landers

Vaughan Rapatahana

with Ngauru Rawiri

Published by Te Perehi o Mātātuhi Taranaki
in association with Lasavia Publishing, (2024).

Te Perehi o Mātātuhi o Taranaki
16 Ōmata Road,Westown, Ngāmotu/New Plymouth
www.matatuhitaranaki.ac.nz

www.lasaviapublishing.com
37 Crescent Road
Waiheke Island
Auckland

ISBN:978-1-991083-06-7
ISSN: 2744-4368 Online
Being Vol.2, No.2 (Dec 2022) and Vol.3, No.1 (March 2023) of
Mātātuhi Taranaki: A Bilingual Journal of Literature.

Acknowledgements

The assistance of the Creative Communities Fund grant from the South Taranaki District Council is gratefully acknowledged. This grant enabled Ngauru Rawiri to verify, emend and check submissions in Te Reo Māori.

We are most grateful to the Waipipi Wind Farm Community Fund administered by Mercury, particularly to their Community Engagement Manager, Kathy Scoular. Their grant ensured the book you now hold was published and was able to be launched in 2023 appropriately. We thank the STDC for assisting with the launch and providing books for schools and authors.

Kupu Whakataki/Foreword

Kia ora tātou rā

Ngā mihi matakuikui nga tāngata o Pātea, Wairoaiti, Waitōtara me Ngamatapouri mā

E harikoa ana ahau, e whakanui ana hoki ahau i te karangatanga mai ki te koha i te kupu o mua ki tēnei pukapuka tino whakamīharo.

Ko tēnei rohe he wāhi ahurea o Taranaki, otirā, ko te tukunga o Poi E nā Māui Dalvanius Prime rāua ko Ngoingoi Pewhairangi me te Karapu Maori o Pātea e noho rongonui tonu ana i roto i ngā hitori o Aotearoa.

Ko tāku whakaaro kia arohaina e ngā kaipānui tēnei pukapuka me te pānui i tētahi atu oriori ia rā. Ka whai whakaaro hou ki te iwi me te whenua.

This book is a fantastic example of what communities can achieve when they are given opportunities to express themselves.

Billed as a literary homage, this collection of poems includes works from established writers such as Janet Hunt, Tony Beyer, Trevor M Landers and Vaughan Rapatahana alongside poems 'harvested' from local primary schools and Pātea Area School.

I suggest readers dip into these pages and savour the fare on offer like a smorgasbord. Alternatively, find a comfy nook and enjoy a sumptuous feast. I congratulate all of the poets here and trust readers will enjoy their work as much as I have.

Rt Hon Adrian Rurawhe
M.P. for Te Tai Hauāuru
Speaker of the House of the Representatives

Hei Tirohanga/Introduction
Ngā Kaiwhakatika The Editors

This publication is a labour of love for us. Vaughan was born in Pātea when the Freezing Works was the largest employer in town. Trevor has had a lifetime affiliation with Waitōtara, based on family associations. We were both determined to see a first-class publication paying literary homage to both places and People. Ngauru provided her expertise in te reo Māori to ensure the submissions we received are grammatically correct and intelligible for readers of Te reo Māori. We have elected to provide translations to make poems in Māori more accessible to a general audience and to encourage learning in te reo rangatira. As editors we share a version of Aotearoa as a bilingual nation enriched by the full experience of culture, language, and world views.

Our vision was to foster a new generations of poetry writers, readers, and admirers. We both know the power of self-expression to not only give testimony to lived experience but Aslo to imagine worlds beyond the limitations of direct experience. Writing poetry can be about declaring truth, but it can be a lot of other things too. Fundamentally, it is a highly imaginative pursuit. We knew that within this catchment area we would uncover lots of new talent and so it proved. We are delighted that so much new poetry-writing talent has been uncovered, assembled, and showcased in this volume.

We also wanted to concentrate pride and reflection in the communities covered by his book. When we started out the naysayers suggested we might get some material for Pātea but would struggle to elicit material from Waverley, Waitōtara, Ngamatapouri and surrounding sub-districts. Indeed, several urged that Trevor and Vaughan would be better off just writing a two-handed work. We rejected that unequivocally. Both Vaughan and Trevor have conducted poetry workshops in the area, and we knew there was talent out there. The extent of that talent has astounded and delighted all of us. Our engagement with these communities proved that not only was there an appetite for poetry, but that we had an obligation to channel that bubbling creativity and to teach people the fundamentals of writing a poem.

The work of Ngauru Rawiri should not be overlooked. As our verifier of works in Te reo Taranaki she has played a vital role, checking sense and grammar, and occasionally providing translations, but always improving the te reo Māori works. Her work has markedly improved the calibre and quality of the writing in Māori.

We believe this is a landmark publication---a first, and one which celebrates Pātea and other localities in the manner they richly deserve! Enjoy! Kia ora koutou katoa.

Ngā Kaiwhakatika/The Editors

Contents

Homage to Waverley   206

Waerea mō te rohe nei

Trevor M. Landers

E ō mātou mātua tūpuna, me tō tātou kaihanga whakaora, manaakitia mai ā tātou piripoho, ā tātou tamariki, me ā rātou mātua, kaitiaki, whanaunga, whānau whānui hoki.

Mā koutou tō mātou ara iraira e whakawātea kia whakatauria rā mō mua ake nei.

Mā koutou ēnei whārangi e whakairia ake ki te taumata, hei mataaho mā mātou e piri ana ki tō Kahurangitanga.

Kia whakatipua ake te puna aroha ki roto ki tēnā o mātou, hei oranga mō te tinana, te hinengaro, te wairua hoki.

Murua ngā tini aitanga a Whiro me mātou hoki e takoia rā. Kia tini kōanga kia hāpaitia, hei whakamāramatia, hei whakatiahotia mā o mātou orangā tū tonu nei.

Homage to Pātea

Towards Tātaraimaka

Vaughan Rapatahana

HERE LIE OVER TWENTY WARRIORS OF
AOTEAROA:
TARANAKI, NGATI RUANUI, WHANGANUI
ME ETEHI ATU.
THEY DIED FOR THEIR BELIEFS
IN THE BATTLE
OF
KATIKARA
4TH JUNE 1863
TAKOTO MAI RATOU I TE RANGIMARIE
ME TE RONGOPAI
O TO TATOU ARIKI.

ERECTED BY THE NEW ZEALAND GOVERNMENT
IN PARTNERSHIP WITH
TE KOTAHITANGA O NGA MAHANGA A TAIRI
JUNE 2002

let there be no white misprision

this was MUCH more

than 'mere skirmish'

this was massacre.

yet another slaughter.

a frisson of blood

for the Pākehā corps.

                                        870 vs 50 or fewer

their conflictual essence

satiated by overkill

replenished by rage

indurate from hate.

                                        870 vs 50 or fewer

carnivalesque for Cameron

glorious for Grey

bombast by Bayly,

a murderer 5

of wounded men.

                                        870 vs 50 or fewer

    &

who stoked the cannon?

    &

who lit the fires

conflagrating

   both

whare & warrior?

                        fewer than 50 vs 870

ngā toa

e tiakina ana

i tō rātau

whenua

mai i te whakaariki kiritea

('On 12 March 1863, 300 men of the 57th Regiment evicted Māori from land
they had occupied at Tātaraimaka, 20 km south-west of New Plymouth.

The five tribes occupying the land – Te Ātiawa, Taranaki, Ngāti Ruanui, Ngāti Rauru and Whanganui – viewed this as an act of war...Grey...[was] planning to evict the 50 Māori who were still camped at Tātaraimaka. On 4 June, 870 men led by the new British commander, Lieutenant-General Duncan Cameron, overwhelmed the small Māori force occupying a pā above the Katikara River, killing half of them. Grey watched with interest from HMS Eclipse, whose heavy guns bombarded the pā from off the coast...It was noted that 'no prisoners were taken' and that at least two wounded Māori were executed'. – University of Waikato, O Neherā)

The Killing of Wounded Men

The first report of the engagement in the *Taranaki Herald* (6 Jun 1863) includes a discussion of British troops killing wounded men.

'There is a question of serious importance to which we wish to call public attention. On what principle are the wounded men and others of the hostile natives who fall into our hands to be treated? It is certain that some at least of those returned as dead in the fight on Thursday would have been among the wounded if the battle had been between two civilized nations; that is to say that some of the wounded Maoris were killed by our men.'

There are also reports in the Wanganui Chronicle from Maori sources of the mistreatment of Maori dead and of some of those killed having been burnt alive (Taranaki Herald 11 Jul 1863).

From: Prickett, Nigel. J. The Military Engagement at Katikara, Taranaki, 4 June 1863,' Records of the Auckland Museum, vol. 45, 2008, pp. 5–41.

[ngā toa

e tiakina ana

i tō rātau

whenua-

the warriors protecting their land

mai i te whakaariki kiritea. -

from the pale invading army].

washing up

Michaela Stoneman

muddy violent cliffs

sluiced chunk by chunk

below into silver

wet swollen river

washing up, frothy

       as a suds-ringed sink

       littered by shells, by weeds

       Neptune's necklace

       salty sea lettuce

       skulking molluscs

a light made up of shadows

she arrived by pungent waves

slapping the shore hard

like daughters' cheeks

when speaking

out of tongue

       she washes up

       rises emphatically towards

       coaxed by currents

      shoving shoulders

      coercing eddies

      licked by whirlpools

      landing sandy crimped

twisted swan neck

throat blue with veins

wrists out, cheesy

gently waterlogged

silky pale cadaver

skin perfect as marble

veins as the river

river as the veins

      clutching charcoal

      from a forgotten fire

      my raisin fingers

      draw her from life

      drenched folds

      suckered buttons

      taught cords

      sea-men knots

      organ crushers

      gripping even tighter

      when wet

I can draw like an
angel after hours
life drawing a cross between
Michelangelo & Colin
McCahon instinctual
to the max perfect
aesthetics incarnate

           mezzotint blacks

           more velvet than antlers

           tide marks

           dark as our voids

           painterly strokes

           perspective

           to die for

she came in
by the river
she left, eventually
by the river.

Wandering around the grounds of Pātea Area School looking for James

Trevor M. Landers

Once again, I marvel, colourful murals

accosting, or at least, surprising an electrician

doing school holiday repairs. It seems it is just me and him

until I meet Kath, the caretaker, who appears to slide

noiselessly out from her cottage, and we have a convivial chat.

Kōrero whakawhitiwhiti, By this time it is plain James has

forgotten about our rendezvous: I will leverage that I say;

Kath grins broadly, bids me *adieu*

a few photographs are taken -- third time will be the charm

    the transformation power of education, whānau

I think as this electric car spirits me noiselessly away,

First, Principals; our first meeting is anticlimactic

In the school hall, James is putting the finishing touches

on an open day; that emerald day of a poetry workshop

with Whaea Ingrid's class; finding a trove of precious gems.

Universal Motors

Gary Bovett

The sign at
    the front
  gives an after-hours number
      there is an eerie silence.

    the blue doors
      securely closed,
        the universe sleeps
    the yellow trim has the effluvium of spy-fi

I wonder if
    they've all gone
      fishing?
The universe celebrates a public holiday.

the gravamen
Vaughan Rapatahana

I looked around the
concise chapel.

you were not there.

outside,
loading the coffin
weighted with gravitas,
I continued to *s c a n*
the tear-torn faces,
those eyes leaking grief.

you were not there.

I gravitate near the telephone.
expecting some avowal;
some concession that your
first-born mokopuna -
was   dead.

no message came.

there have been none since.

only this gravamen
wrenched
from within my soul:

you were **never** there.

it was as if
we were mere
remora,
nibbling nugatory
on your
more substantial
self.

burdened with your being;
a   l   w   a   y   s
attending,

yet
forever
flailing
in your

absence.

The Menstrual Blues
Name Withheld

Like a crimson wave
flows through the sea
there are sublime mysteries
hidden under a skirt.
Narrating in great detail
& in a blurry way
the intensity of renewal
withers the sense of control
it seeps away tear shaped.
Cycle of curses and expletives
screaming and complaining
completely defeats you
and you fall lying where you are
luckily it only lasts a few days.

Kiwis against seabed mining (Waipipi 2017)

Christine Broughton

South Taranaki seabed has been brought,
    our Iwi fight still goes on,
        is this history repeating itself,
            with others claiming something.
                it doesn't seem wrong!?
They took our land now
    they want our sand.
        Moana Jackson wrote Colonisation is "an attack
        on the indigenous soul."
            Here in Taranaki, hegemony continues to roll.
            Thirty-five years they say they will be grounding
        the drill, at least it's not one hundred and seventy
    years, but still.

Impacting us, Māori,
        with colonisation just wasn't enough,
            at least the sharks and fishes
                can get away from this stuff.
            What of our kai moana, will it still be there?
                I personally don't think they even care.

The Iwi, our guardians preparing to fight,

      taking this to the high court to do what is right.

      Our tamariki ---who are now feeling the bite,

        what is their future? Is it looking bright?

    Our future is their future, and we want it to be fair,

  but with this land mining the fish will not be there.

The hegemony battle is bringing the community together as they say:

    "We are in this together to fight to the end,

we are realising how important it is to have you as our friends."

    The closeness this

      to put up a fight to continue till all is done.

Te porotēhi mō te takutai moana

Kua hokona atu te takutai moana o
Taranaki ki te tonga,
Ka whawhai tonu tō mātou
iwi,
E whakaauau ana anō tēnei hītori
peange, ko ētehi atu o rātou e kii ana ,
ehara i te mea he hē.

I raupatungia e rātou tō mātou whenua, kāti
rā ināinei e hiahia ana ki tō mātou onepū
hoki.
Hei tā Moana Jackson, ko te tāmitanga te
tukitukia o te wairua taketake'
i Taranaki nei, ka haere tonu te
whakatuanui a te karauna.
Toru tekau mā rima ngā tau tā rātou e kii ana
ka oreorea i te takutai,
ehara i te kotahi rau whitu tekau tau,
erangi tonu.
Ka whakaaweawetia mai ki a mātou te
iwi Māori, ehara mā te tāmitanga e whakaea
Waimarie ngā mako me ngā ika e taea

te kauhoe atu kia wātea atu i ēnei hara.

ka pēhea tā tātou kaimoana, ka ora tonu ki reira?
Ki au nei, ehara tā rātou i te kumanu.

ko ngā iwi, ko ō mātou kaitiaki, e
whakarite ana mō te whawhai, ka haria tēnei
take ki te kooti matua hei whai i ngā mahi tika,
ko ā maatou tamariki, kei a rātou te maemae
ināianei,
ka pēhea ā rātou anamata? Ka pīata tonu
mai?

Ko tā mātou anamata tā rātou anamata, ā, e
hiahia ana mātou
kia tika, erangi nei ka oreore whenua tonu, ka
ngaro atu ngā ika katoa.
nā te whawhai whakatuanui mātou o te
hapori e karapoti nei anā, ko tā rātou e kī
ana, kei a mātou te mana kia tū kotahi kia
whawhai ki te mutunga,
kei te mōhio hoki mātou he mea nui te
piri ki a koutou hei hoa mā mātou
Koinei te tikanga o te kōpipiri, kia whawhai
tonu ka tika, kia meingatia.2

---

2 Translation support provided by the editors.

Summertime at the Pātea Motor Camp

Zoie Parmenter

Grass blanched by a fiercer sun to brittle brown
iron sands scorching underfoot a hasty hot-footed retreat
driftwood serves as rampart and respite from seared soles
the river sparkles catchment champagne into the Bight
red-cheeked campers wrestle crinkly awnings open wide
empty bottles of cheap plonk discarded like slain marines
mid-morning shower and ablutions & the towel kaleidoscope
lines of panties and t-shirt hung like semaphore flags
the comforting milieu of summertime at the PMC.

Ironsand Walks

Zoie Parmenter

An exclamation mark
    to a year of quietly spoken expletives
      we peel the onion of the unsaid
    soothing words on crashing waves
      footprints disappearing
in shimmering sands of iron.

This year, as in the recent past
    to this beachfront asylum
      the strains of living are consigned
    slipped in a tight bikini,
      a pair of bulging swimming trunks
    waiting in vain for a Polaroid camera.

In the warm summer evenings
    we unravel each other
with wine indecently gulped &
      inopportune clothes flung to sandy floors
    the tang of coitus and salt flaring our nostrils
      the distant rumbling of the sea.

as I lose another
Vaughan Rapatahana

the discontinuation
    continues.
an ex-lover
eschewing suicide watch,
her scarred wrists
palimpsests of pain.

a former friend,
hacking his
emphysemic path
toward quietus.

veteran uncles,
war-torn whanaunga
flensed of fear,
too aged to linger
    longer.
all metamorphosing
as they traverse

the orphic threshold

between bardo and beyond.

karakia

wane after a while,

slip away like

unguent fingertips,

like your grip on mine.

that last gasp,

those occluded eyes,

your body

a thin earthquake.

the uroboric void

replete

once more,

as I lose another.

Why pamper life's complexities when the leather runs smooth on the passenger seat? (On the mole, Pātea).

Name Withheld

This poem

had its gestation in joy

it bore a genial smile

was noted for its jovial countenance

people remarked at its elan and exuberance

the vivacity of expression

frothing like a gently perturbed jereboam of champagne

or a double decomposition,

the unheralded exultations of chemical reactions--

like the gaiety of neurotransmitters

embracing the ecstasies of endorphins

after the rapture of vigorous lovemaking

the delectation of the post-coital regalement

but we know the cyclicity of the seasons

that there is a time for this

and a time for that.

The abasement started imperceptibly

with his job---more travel, longer hours, opportunities,

I felt the slow movement of tectonic plates

creating the cleft that would become the abyss

the unfathomable Mariana Trench of the soul,

Thrown into an ungovernable fissure

a chasm so vertiginous that my miraculous extrication

discombobulated even me; stood for days flabbergasted.

Our holiday to Guam and the North Marianas

is not a lingering chancre, a suppurating wound

as I gaze out at the spiteful seascape from the Mole

'wondering then, what would peace of mind be like?

Doleful, disconsolate and dispirited

The sea sometimes feels like my only friend, a tidal ally

the love dissolved as if by sea

the melancholy of shrieking gulls

the maudlin sky a miserable *mis-en-scene*

the detritus washed ashore is not helping

my heart is disintegrating.

On the concrete cubes of the mole

even the resplendent green algae in the cracks

takes on an ominously derisive tone

the sea loves the intoning of inconsolability

ebbing and flowing, swirling and swelling at the mouth.

The dilapidated pier is a leitmotif of perditions & decrepitude

lost moorings and a love cast irretrievably adrift

in the riptide of the swift-winged channel

fodder for pipi, barnacles and periwinkles

sluicing a nutrient swap out into the Bight.

A farrago of cars now; parked up

contemplative and connubial---no resentment here.

The leather runs smooth on the passenger seat.

In the area
Craig Foltz

Car-

After becoming beached the vessel becomes
A compass & is left out in the sun. Lathered
In shark oil & stuffed with flax fibre. An aspect
That's rectangular, jive, freezing & penguin-
Based. Shortly after the turn-off to Waitōtara
We intermingled with life on this planet. As
For the foreshore, this is not how one should
Navigate the matrix. Oh, to send the cipher
Running in all directions! Oh, to mix blood
With sacred ceremonies. This is how the song
Hit number 1. This is how we extracted every
Last memory from Waipipi. Mention this sparse
Wilderness at your own peril. I remember the way
You looked when you looked back but I can't
Recall the name.

- Lyle

I roto i te rohe
Craig Foltz

Car-

whai muri i te taunga ki uta ka noho te waka

He kāpehu kua waiho ki te rā. Kua pania

mā te hinu mango, kua kapi ki te muka harakeke.

He āhua tapawhā, he hiwi, ka whakamātao ka whakakororātia

I muri tata i te hurihanga ki Waitōtara

I whakauruuru mātou ki te oranga o tēnei ao.

Mō te takutai moana, ehara i te mea me pēnei ai

te whakatere i te poukapa.

Aue, ki te tuku i te uhingaro,

E rere ana i ngā huarahi katoa!

Aue, ki te whakaranu i te toto

Me ngā kawa tapu.

Koia te waiata i patua te nama 1.

Koinei te ara i kapohia e mātou

Te mahara whakamutunga mai Waipipi.

Kia whakahuatia tēnei koraha tūrukiruki

Ki tō ake mōrearea

Ka mahara āhau ki tō āhua

I a koe i tiro whakamuri mai erangi tē taea au

Whakamaharatia te ingoa.

- Lyle.[3]

---

[3] Te reo Māori translation by Trevor M. Landers.

Love Story: Call and Response
Mike Oliver Johnson and Trevor M. Landers

Love Story, by Mike Johnson

you are the line
I am the colour

you are the form
I am the afterimage

you are the shutter
I am the plate

you are the brush
I am the vista

you are the cut
I am the content

we are
each to the other
as the other
together

be it hourglass or mirror[4]

---

[4] 'Love Story' was first published in Tarot, vol.1, (December 2020),

Response, by Trevor M. Landers

You are the passing lanes leaving Pātea
I am the colours of the Pātea Māori club billboard

You are the serenity of a seascape at Manu Bay
I am the aftermath of a howling southerly storm.

You are the shutters of a shop married to dereliction
I am the photographer of bold dreams evanescing

You are the environmentally conscious murals on Egmont St
I, the dreamer singing lullabies to the Gods of Transformation

You are poem lifted off the page with cadence & gusto
I am the poem who harbours silent dreams refusing death

we are
one to the other
master and apprentice
joined by letters

be it Waiheke or Waitōtara
palimpsest or paradox
it is love and affection all around.

Trevor thanks Mike for his co-operation and generosity in let this
collaboration take place under blind conditions for him.

He Iwi Tahi Tātou

Airana Ngarewa

Papa was no mother to them, the koroua warned. Tāne no tūpuna. They know no kinship with us, the hau kāinga of these rich lands. Even those well-meant mihingare have become little more than brokers of property, the most crooked among them negotiating plots enough to feed whole hapū. Whakarongo mai e te iwi. The veil of partnership has been lifted, and the Treaty had been revealed a Trojan Horse. Hobson's pledge was not an expression of unity but violent assimilation. He iwi (ko)tahi tātou indeed.

An Imaginarium: The Pier at Pou o Turi

Anonymous

Sunstruck spray sifts back the gray mole

out in the flange of the river mouth

muddy brackwater fans out

a diffusion of up-river deforestation

the nitrogen leaching, toxic algae blooming

and still they argue they are not to blame.

Or rather they spurn accountability

responsibility means acknowledging there is a problem.

Farmers, more protected than bloody flora and fauna.

So could we slalom through the wooden legs of the pier

whose encrustations skewer kindred fish at high tide

& on horsehair horizons pencil-line galloping eyes

the bareback bravado like a scene from Waipiro Bay.

The dressage horse obliges with a figure of eight

then off sluggishly over the sinking sandhills

with shrieks of self-conscious mirth, that Māori boy

as the air heals the wound salt rubbed.

On the Mole, X, the unknown woman,

statuesque and shapely, striding out sensuously

a buxom beauty who is a figment of imagination

the mocked indignation, the opprobrium, I get it it

but e-quality means these secret private pleasures are not

the preserve of small retinues of unimpeachable women, surely?

This glamazon has gyre, her gait enthrals, it is a reverie, an

imaginarium, men and women do this all the time in chambers

--No one was harmed in the making and retelling of this poem.

There is no polka-dotted parasol or Jane Austen affectations

there is a measureless littoral idyll

the spite of salt peppering a light zephyr

shingle and sand and a strand of three ballerina gulls

precariously balancing on one leg;

Nature loves bluster & braggadocio

Behold the tarāpuka: ultimate ruffler and rodomont

moves the lesser gulls on. It is what we do: moving on.

Untitled

Pasha Clothier

Today I saw again the mountain
brooding over humanity's passage
through rites of existence

And I was moved strangely
by words falling
wind soft and specific
snowflakes wistfully dancing
in the drifting breeze

Through pound and whisper
raindrops pock the river erudite
flowing from nature's tongue

Crowned by a deep white crop of clouds,
thermally soars a pathos sonorous of the ocean home
that is the collective heart

My dogs
Ingrid Frengley-Vaipuna

Beach glistening
sun low tide low
dots in the distance
sniffing, absorbing everyone
since high tide.
Smell trumps all.

PAS Students Off to Uni

Ingrid Frengley-Vaipuna

Excited, determined

future shaping but

afraid of life with others

their mess, their germs, their difference, their bad habits.

Te Reo calling back to ancient genes

overrides the fear of stepping out

....and away!

A Pātea View on COVID

Ingrid Frengley-Vaipuna

Breathe/panic subsiding slowly/air warming behind the mask
unnaturally/worlds shrinking walls/border/ new glass ceilings
as a new enemy permeates/the very air that sustains us/ Fear of
breathing in/shapes new ways of relating.

Day 3 – Sat 28 March 2020
Michaela Stoneman

Walking the dogs to the domain
to sniff and piss and run

two cars pass
sedan carrying a woman alone

white ute with a big white dog
I remember how spooky the domain

at dusk or dark
can be sometimes.

Within the blur, mud, fog
faceless terrors crouch there

Staring fiercely through the gloom
there is just so much to be terrified by

All these small fears lurking
I notice the difference

Between the greens of grass
Kikuyu is the freshest hue

Without it this town
would simply blow away.

Tomato Stall

Hannah Oliver

I pass it
Every time I drive by

decelerating southward
revving up heading north

I have thought of stopping
devouring some juicy reds

Initially it was $5 per bag
With inflation, now $7

Little tomato stall
I shall return.

A 16th Birthday Party in Whenuakura
Te Tuhi Holdsworthy

Troy and Ramon knew they had a distinct advantage,
both members of a local first XV, accustomed to
grog-guzzling; Arnie, Simon, and Paul---at a distinct
disadvantage: experience, frequency, successive sessions.
Our boys arrive, are feed and annex the lounge room,
howls of protest from otherwise adorable sister, ruled
inadmissible. Five hours of semi-witty banter followed,
drinking games spin from elevated merriment to clear
inebriation. All camped on the front lawn.
The infirm and intoxicated not tempted to foolishly drive away.
The keg plumbed, the drinking and bravado commenced.
Troy, Ramon and Simon fared better by experience, luck, or
......Arnie and Paul were driven to complete insensibility much
to the amusement of the slightly more sober troika----because
no-one was sober.
The scoreboard morphing into *vomitus spectacularum*.
Each held the hangover of a boisterous Frenchman in the
morning. Life lesson about knowing your limits and subtle
peer pressure. Troy would become a Lecturer, public servant
and now hardly drinks. Ramon, enjoys a good tipple with his
missus, just make it *Tui*. Simon, farming in Central, his palate

improved immeasurably one suspects.

Paul is local, can hold his own I imagine, a good joker.

Arnie spent time in Africa, and the Armed Forces, so increased capacities shifted, and may yet remain

Sadly, Mark, who was meant to come, and didn't

and ever more tragically, much, much later

committed suicide, such a ghastly and senseless waste, in a slough of despair.

I dredge this up not show how inebriated our adolescent ways may have been but to honour our host Arnie, and his family & to remember Mark, with kindliness and sincerity.

I think of them often, as I am sure the others do.

I so wish he had come that night.

stayed with us to make deeper memories.[5]

---

[5] EDITOR'S NOTE: A rite of passage poem will signal a significant event taking place in someone's life. A rite of passage is an important ceremony or a life changing event. Thus, we can infer that the poem's meaning will be important and serious. Friendship or mateship poems are older than the hills and a recurrent literary trope, emphasising the importance of friendship, manaakitangi, Freundlich, etc by highlighting solidarity, emotional connections, shared experiences or rupture, loss, and grief. In fact, the whole kaleidoscope of human emotion. Teen poems either describe teenage experience, or provide an outlet for adults to revisit the past. Angst is common though not mandatory. Poems dealing with Depression, school, friends love, family and the teenage experience are common. 'Daddy' by Sylvia Plath is infamous for her no-holds critique of her father and their troubled relationship during her adolescence and beyond. See: https://www.poetryfoundation.org/poems/48999/daddy-56d22aafa45b2 (Accessed 4 February 2021).

The Power of Education Mural at PAS

Orlando Davidson

Mural at Pātea Area School   © Trevor M. Landers (December 2021)

Upon the wall it waits for a reader as people pass unaware.
The common do not much care.
To some it is colourful art.
To others, a school project and a vivid mural alive with colour.
Others find words of expansion and enlargement and more!
Some, simply material; but it has a fabulous purpose
for those who look and read and absorb!
Like a page in a book, a map or a pathway leading us onward.
To those savvy few, see what a thing can mean, and it can do.
The power lies within it and within you too
The great transformer: education lies in you.

Observances at the Bridge Dairy

Jah'Quasha Katene

The cars, they come and go, come and go
Parked up at the Bridge Dairy like boats

Aunty goes into the shop for milk
Comes out with two loaves of bread and vegemite

Uncle Bob goes into the shop for tampons
Comes out with two ply toilet paper

Te Raahui goes into the dairy for a sugar-free Coke
She bounds of the store with a Moro bar too

Koro shuffles into the shop looking for fly spray
Cool! He gets it, and a newspaper under his arm.

Taranaki Oceans: Kaua e tumutumu te ara moana i Taranaki

Miley Davidson

Mural on Egmont St, Pātea.   © Trevor M. Landers, (October 2021).

Kaua e tumutumu te ara moana i Taranaki

Desist from interfering with the oceans of Taranaki

The oceans of Taranaki, such beautiful things, being put to waste, used as a dump, an "unlimited" food resource, instead of being cared for; admired. The oceans are not ours; no one owns them, we have to right to put refuse in the great blue; there are timeless treasure we care for them on behalf of future generations. We need to save, preserve, and protect not just for today, but tomorrow, and future people as yet unborn. No pollutants in Taranaki oceans. We can do better Taranaki.

A Happy Earth Poem

A Student at St. Joseph's School, Pātea

I just want the earth to be happy
for the land not to cry
like rivers in flood
for our oceans
to be clean and clear
so dolphins, whale and fish
can play.
My koko says he swam in the river as a boy
I thought it was fibbing
but it was cleaner then he said
it was not as dirty as now
I would not think of swimming it
& my koko says neither would he
I just want the earth to be happy
it is the only place we can live.

Manu Bay, Pātea, © Trevor M. Landers (February 2022).

At Manu Bay

Marley Ranginui-Hurley, Stephanie Ratahi, Hamuera Wallace-Davis, Raheel Rio, Carlos Hippolite, John Muncaster and Trelise Kingi-Karaitiana.

Rush hour at Manu Bay; a single set of footprints, a fun place for families to frolic; playing fetch with excitable dogs, precious moments at the beach, making memories, collecting seashells by the seashore, the waves crashing in, contemplation of a swim, scanning for sharks. Some launch surfboards or cast off for Kahawai; tonight's kai for the whānau. Further on, sandcastles are hurriedly constructed as we chase crabs darting for cover. The relentless in and out breaths of the tide, like a weary old man sighing after exertions.

The Authors, St Josephs School, Patea, July 2022

Not the Ballad of McCarty and Hunger

Tatiana Thomas

McCarty & Hunger Ltd, est 1878 © Trevor M. Landers

(January 2022)I conjure the Lewis and Clark expedition
After the Louisiana Purchase, a trek north for water.

I hum to the comforting melody of Simon and Garfunkel
For bridging troubled waters in an orange kayak.

I titter to the irreverent comedy of that Mitchell and Webb look
Sardonic humour flavours the surreality of dystopian times.

I convulse at the vaudeville japing of Laurel and Hardy,
a salutary reminder to cherish the medicine of silliness.

Perhaps you long for the panache of Starsky and Hutch
racing after seventies villains in supercharged sports cars.

Or would rather carp and cavil like Statler and Waldorf
peering down at the world sneering at the insanity of it all?

Should we listen to the ballads of Lennon and McCartney?
The soundtrack of a vastly different age and era.

This is not exactly the ballad of Hunger and McCarty
But we can marvel surely at their stickability & longevity.

The Fading Grandeur of the Old Pātea Post and Telegraph Building

Tatiana Thomas and Trevor Landers

Old Post and Telegraph Office, Pātea, © Trevor M. Landers
(January 2022)

Buildings are people
their conception is more laboured

more planning and consent
less left to chance,

whim or impetuosity
rendered to the margins.

During the budding infancy
construction follows exactitude,

no tantrums and temperamentality
each brick is adolescent challenge.

In adulthood, serviceability and function,
The licking of stamps, the languor of queues.

The fading grandeur of this old lady now,
neglected as she leans on a Zimmer frame

Telegraph office struck by obsolescent silences
There she sits in an avenue of neglect, façade slipping.

This grand old dame may outlast us both, graves beckoning,

potent symbol: an aeon being lost to decrepitude & memory.

Patea Maori Club's hit Poi E immoralised on a billboard at the Northern end of town, © Trevor M. Landers, 10 October 2021

The Pātea Māori Club

Trevor M. Landers

Everyone knows Poi E,

      written by Ngoi Pēwhairangi

     No.1 in 1984, and charting in each

        of the succeeding three decades

     the iconic video

     irrepressible: Dalvanius Prime

   the ubiquitous chihuahua, his Wyandotte chickens

     his much larger than life ebullience,

typically picaresque Māui:

trickster, musician, impresario

the purple palace making a splash.

The crushing closure Freezing Works derelict now

RIP: 1883-1982; in 1933 employing 1000+ men

when the British Vestey Group cut and ran

scattering whānau to the four winds in search of work,

many club members gone, but still:

a spirit-lifter, the song, the album, the Tiki-tour of the

UK: London Palladium

the Edinburgh Festival,

& a peroration at the Royal Command Performance

after another every-week rehearsal

at the whare, past the Garden of Tutunui, on Bedford.

Poi E

Maui Dalvanius Prime, Ngoi Pēwhairangi and the Pātea Māori Club

E rere ra e taku poi porotiti
Tītahataha ra, whakararuraru e
Porotakataka rā, poro hurihuri mai
Rite tonu ki te tiwaiwaka e

Ka parepare ra, pīoioi a
Whakahekeheke, e kia korikori e
Piki whakarunga ra, ma muinga mai a
Taku poi porotiti, taku poi e!

Poi E, whakatata mai
Poi E, kaua he rerekē
Poi E, kia piri mai ki au
Poi E, e awhi mai ra
Poi E, tāpekatia mai.

Poi E, ō tāua aroha -
- Poi E - paiheretia ra.
POI... TAKU POI, E!

Swing out rhythmically, my feelings
lean out beside me, so deceptively.
Swing round and down, spin towards me
just like a fantail.

Swing to the side: swing to and fro
zoom down, wriggle,
climb up above, swarm around me
my whirling emotions, my poi, Yeah!

Oh my feelings, draw near,
Oh my poi, don't go astray
Oh my affections, stick to me
Oh my instincts, take care of me
Oh my emotions, be entwined around me.

Oh poi, our love...
Oh poi ...binds.
Poi.... my poi, yeah!

Ngoi Pēwhairangi with Dalvanius Prime (1982)
© Te Papa (D Prime Collection)

Note: Poi-E had a germinal beginning in Ruatoria in 1982. Dalvanius was playing a gig there in between Te reo Māori studies at what was then Wellington Polytechnic when linguist Ngoi Pēwhairangi asked musician Maui Dalvanius Prime how he would teach the younger generation to be proud of being Māori and Kiwi. He told her he could do it by giving them their language and culture through the medium they were comfortable with. Dalvanius later said:

> I went to visit her and we hit it off," he said. "She said the only way you'll learn about the Māori language is if you stick around on the marae and come with me.

The rest is, as they say, is splendid history and a filip for the burgeoning Mā.[6]

---

[6] We are indebted to the Pātea Māori Club, the Maui Dalvanius Prime Trust and the Pēwhairangi whānau for their assistance and support . See: https://folksong. org.nz/poi_e/ (Accessed 10 September 2022).

Te Māra o Tutunui

Vaughan Rapatahana

The Garden of Tutunui, © Trevor M. Landers, (January 2022).

This photo shows the Garden of Tutunui, a large sculpture of a whale skeleton designed by Kim Jarrett in 2006. It was permanently installed at Pātea in 2009.

What is the background to this installation?

In Māori tradition, the great Taranaki chief Tinirau fell out with his tohunga, Kae, over the chief's pet whale, Tutunui.

Tinirau offered his whale to his guest, Kae, to transport him back to his own village. (Kae had tasted the whale flesh and wanted to keep and then eat Tutunui for himself!)

Indeed, Kae killed and ate the whale. So Tinirau sent a waka filled with wāhine in a kapa haka group, to Kae's village. Before they left, Tinirau's youngest sister asked him, "What are the marks by which we shall know Kae?" and he answered her, "Oh, you cannot mistake him, his teeth are uneven, and all overlap one another." They would have to make Kae laugh to view the teeth.

It took a while for Kae to even smile, but because their performance was so irresistible Kae did smile widely, revealing his distinctive overlapping teeth and sealing his fate. Death!

Another bloody freezing works poem
Tony Beyer

in those days
what I'd describe
as an old man

was one probably
twenty years younger
than I am now

white boiler suit
sweaty felt hat
shuffling into the canteen

knees buggered
back buggered
hearing gone

in the daylong
shrieking clash
of shackles

grizzling about
the stockyard boys
pinching roast spuds

out of the warmer
where he'd left them
for smoko

last horse
a tailender
last pay pissed away

eyes a
faded blue
like winter mist

waiting for the whistle
that says home
when you have to go

Roots

Mark Pirie

(in.memoriam. Maui Dalvanius Prime, 1948-2002)

The irrepressible Maui Dalvanius Prime,
c.1970s flamboyance, © SST

Dalvanius dies. At least it's made
the news. 'He was a Maori joker
wasn't he?' a man says reading aloud.

I think back to the '80s. Where was
I when the Pātea Māori Club topped
the charts? Somewhere near Hāwera
I think, visiting my Great Aunt, or in
Stratford on a trip, moving down those
long wide streets of dairy town,
working class New Zealand, and unaware
of the frigid existence of many.
Now, older, it comes back in the form
of Dalvanius's corpse. The last of '80s
Kiwiana perhaps. Another icon
dipping down like the cattle flung dung
or that typically local tele-setting country sun.

mayhem

Vaughan Rapatahana

te aneatanga/mayhem.
he kupu tika.
iwi massacring iwi with muskets.

te tīrangorango/mayhem.
tētahi atu kupu tika.
Pākehā decimating iwi with disease.

te kaumingomingo/mayhem.
he kupu tino tika.
coronavirus exterminating masses with ease.

such a futile waste of life/
he oranga huakore, he moumou.
derisible/
tika tō tātou hahani.

we require comity/te whakaute.
not mayhem/ehara i te whakahārangi.

ehara i āpōpō,
but today.
ināianei

[he kupu tika – a true word
tētahi atu kupu tika – another true word
he kupu tino tika – a very true word
ehara i te āpōpō – not tomorrow
ināianei – now]

Stopping for Ice-cream in Pātea

Martyn Brown

Trevor says

it is part of the local tikanga

to stop for ice-cream in Pātea

so that is what we do

licking furiously

as the cream liquifies into streams

cascading down our shirts

like many sweet-toothed fools before us.

A Freezing Works Lament

Trevor M. Landers and Veronika Vovchuk

The old Freezing Works, © Trevor M Landers August 2022

I often pull in here for a few moments' respite
a tranquil place to nibble a ham sandwich, sluice a drink
to check up on the dilapidated old girl, her tattered skirts
gently listing into the river like a Soviet anachronism.

Today, the river is in flood, wet-knickered
an orgasm of muddy froth engulfing the banks
rotting the old piers, discolouring the piles
feint traces of industry washing away daily.

The skeleton stands stoic like an abandoned *Sanhedrin*
an old gunslinger oblivious to its own death
stuck in the place when the fatal shots rang out
skin now canvas for daubers and taggers.

The air is pungent with the ghosts of slain cattle
in many ways the silence is more foreboding
former cool stores as an erstwhile *konzentrationlager*
no longer the earthy gallows humour of the slaughtermen.

With each visit, memories are cauterised like hide
bleak genuflections to the disappearing past
the tattered gospel of industrial decays
barbed wire portrait of a time long extinguished.

I am here as a grotesque biographer of (un)closure
a ghoulishly macabre forensic autopsy of cessation
places where gooseflesh kisses now snatched by coy teens
the severed edge of serrated dreams, a festered eyesore.

Raumano

Gaenor Brown

"Freezing Works at Pātea
That's just what you'll be aftah
Coming 'ere from Wales you say
Golden days gone forevah!"

I reject imprisonment
by structures patriarchal
tell my story as I want
tell you what is what:

> looking for a place to film
> a version of *The Visit*[7]
> NZ place with history
> Not Europe, like in Guellen

bringing all my UK shit
for a bit of alchemy
here comes creativity
irony of colony

---

[7] By Friedrich Durrenmatt

explained intended *mise en scene:*

a building's sad demise

once glorious and thriving

now consigned to ruin

All this for a film they ask

What's it meant to mean?

funny you should ask I quip

it's all about my dream

to be the best director

shoot all the winning shots

show freezing workers' glory

But what about Turi's dream?

Though nightmared long ago

There's traces in the waka

And in the river too- of wealth

Beyond the fabric

Beyond the mortared brick

Beyond unworthy capital

In a thousand leaves

Listen Wales

You should know better

Hear a cacophonic whoomp?

The sound of *cyrch*, the sound of selling.[8]

Your story isn't freezing works

    and wealth in degradation

        It's about some people broken,

            scattered

                like a thousand leaves.

---

[8] Cyrch is Welsh for onslaught or raid. The opening verse is in Englyn Cyrch - an old Welsh or Cornish quatrain - 7 syllables per line with rigid rhyme patterns.

Te Rauhui's Epic Poem
Names Withheld

Poems are like burbling babies
    they need attentive parents
    they clamour for engrossment
    they demand skilful thoughtfulness
        but not every act of supreme imagination
      leads to a bounteous conception
this business requires patience and repetition
      application to the taste
        these babies cry and mourn neglect
          they cry for their māmā, lament for their pāpā
      only on the page or in recital do they sing life.

This intimated poem was conceived and delivered
      in Whaea Ingrid's classroom
    a beautiful embodiment of Te Tiriti
        reo e rua, a bilingual manifestation
  in real time Jah'Quasha and others
      beholden to this remarkable birth; an arrival
        perfect just as it was, full of promise & portent
      a child of te ao hurihuri
        a beautiful expression of life and hopefulness.

He mea whakamīharo tō whiti
me noho ki tēnei whārangi
I a au e pānui ana ka kite i te kanapa
Ka mōhio au, he kotiro pai ki te tuhituhinga
Ka pīata mai tō anamata
me tuku whiti koe ki Mātātuhi Taranaki
www.matatuhitaranaki.ac.nz
I ngā wā katoa!
Kōrero atu ki ō hoa anō

Ka taea e tātou te kōrero mārie
Ka tangi te mate o tēnei tamaiti
Kaore i tupu ake i runga i ēnei whārangi
E tika ana mō te oranga whakamīharo
engari ka hoatu e mātou ki a koe i tēnei whakanui
He rotarota e mau ana i tō ingoa
kaore i tuhia e koe engari i tuhia ki a koe
ehara i te mea whakamīharo pēnei i tō tuhituhinga
engari nei he tohu nā mātou ki te oranga o tō pepi
Ka hiahia mātou, te māmā me tō tamaiti.
He oranga roa me te harikoa tonu rā.

no massacre in 'our' country

Vaughan Rapatahana

they do not teach massacre,
in their schools.
they never will.

i kōhurutia ngā Māori

you prate,
'our history syllabus
has been reviewed,
will be renewed,
we will incorporate,
what really happened'.

i kōhurutia ngā Māori

I state, 'bullshit.

Handley's Woolshed is unknown,
Rangiaowhia will not be mentioned,
Ōrākau will remain ignored.
Tātaraimaka will be sequestered as skirmish,
and Ngatapa
won't even garner a glance'.

i kōhurutia ngā Māori

they do not teach massacre,
in their schools.
they never will.

[i kōhurutia ngā Māori – Māori were massacred]

Waiata o te waka Aotea

Mercedes Webb-Pullman

Look! A canoe that will never float,
nomad roaming a grey car park,
oars unmoving, flecking your skin
with broken droplets of foam
like ancient tears for a son killed and eaten
tears for a family torn apart
when angry blood had spoken.

Approach close on a moonlit night
and hear ancient sailors moaning
of homelands and hearts and harvests
of blood and soil and burgeoning seeds
of Turi the captain and Rongorongo his wife
and remember the seed will never be lost
that's sown from Rangiātea.

'Aotea Waka Stop', © Trevor M. Landers (September 2021)

A Typically Kiwi Experience

Jessica Pourchi Ruiz with Trevor M. Landers

If you were to ask a foreigner just like me

what is a true Kiwi experience

they would probably declare a visit to a holy cathedral of rugby:

an All Blacks Test and the haka.

And if you want an even more Kiwi experience

watch the same game down at the pub in Pātea

and behold the theatre of the locals

it is an anthropological feast

that will linger long in the warmest memories.

when the utu came

Vaughan Rapatahana

'Until the lions have their own historians, the history of the hunt will always glorify the hunter' ----Chinua Achebe.

when the utu came
it was hypnogogic,
like those   gaudy   paintballs
          behind   your   eyes,
when you rub too hard.

when the utu came,
you had earned it.
merely by remaining caustic
awake   & somewhat aware.

your pen had done the dirty work:
it was up to readers
to scan intense
your sensate words,

to flit the message

on to designated others

simply by flicking the page

in their directions.

when the utu came

night-calling in its

open-mouthed finger-gibe

they knew,   as

                                  they had

always known,

they would wake as pariah,

pale castrato fingers snatching

at the jaunty sands

of shores no longer stolen –

if they ever woke at all.[9]

---

[9] Utu is best thought of a reciprocal cost, a reparation or recompense, based on activities and relationships, though it is sometimes importunately defined as revenge.

Seaward and Syphilitic: An Imaginarium[10]
Dennis Litchwark

I was brought here

on a barque

to the Pātea Mole

when once they dreamed

this place would be

the capital of the new colony.

        Come this way, my friends,

        my chamber of horrors beckons

        You will not want to gaze,

        but you must, my friends, you must

        I am the colour of colonialism past.

Behold the ceramic jars of rum

my silver tongue

the storm of pornographic pestilence

Yes, merchants of filth, purveyors of slime

---

[10] WRITER"S NOTE: I am indebted to Trevor Landers for his suggestion for the title, to remind people that this is an imaginative work designed to encourage people to think about the complexities of a fictionalised meeting between Māori and Pākehā. It is definitely not written to offend anyone.

violate the sanctity of the nethers

So that the obscenity in my extremity

may cross the threshold of your whare.

        The brown wrapper

        The brown sugar

        I have a taste for it

        odious that I am

        I wrench my scrotum,

        cloak a place where lewdness

        and lasciviousness begin

        to warp the minds of your

        beloved wāhine

        some of them only children

So be brave,

my friends, I am a chamber of horrors

Lay your eyes on exhibit me

I arrived at the Mole

on a coastal-faring barque

and I will not leave

until I am whakapapa.

Still not Finnished re-defining Pātea
Tanja Tahvanainen

Pātea could be a sort of food, a pâté, a spread smeared on crackers. Or a benevolent father. Or the antonym of pathetic. Is paint, like a patina, or a *meisterwerk*. Pātea is art in itself.

coloratura

Vaughan Ratapahana

be kind to your younger self.
they did not know.
be forgiving
of their foolish acts.

the ideals
deliquesced,
the hopes
submerged
by the seiche
of cynicism.

the bonds
busted,
the alliances
seized gelid
in the chill
of decennaries.

love
who you once were.
be generous
to that former self,
in a coloratura
to that unversed mimic
no longer gazing back
from the mirror.

Bibliothèque du Communauté de Pātea

Trevor M. Landers

The Old Pātea Library, circa 1930, © Trevor M. Landers, (October 20210

Ko te whare pukapuka te pokapū o te ao pohewa:
La bibliothèque, est la pièce
maîtresse de la culture,
montre-moi tes bibliothèques et tes orateurs, et mon cœur va chanter.
A library can be the centre of culture
& learning; show me your orators and your libraries

and my heart will sing.
Te Whare Pukapuka Āpitihanga ā Pātea is sleeker, modern,
 a larger footprint, air-conditioned
 with modern accoutrements
 myriad utilitarian benefits--- I get it.
Gazing upon the Old Pātea Library
 with its Spanish mission-style clock
British racing green louvres,
 terracotta roof, pulley and sash windows
 even a petite-faux balcony, Doric columns,
the needless ornamentation,
 oh, sublime brickwork!
 I think we must weave the past and future
Donne-moi un livre
 et je te montrerai le nouveau monde
give me a book, & I will show you the world.
Homai ki au tētehi pukapuka
 ka whakaatu angeau ki a koe i te ao hou.

Tūrangawaewae

Ingrid Frengley-Vaipuna

(As I read Church's 'Heartland of Aotea'
absorbing more of the murky history
of this place and its people
I realise)

The longest I've ever lived anywhere is here
where, living quietly, within a decaying mansion
and ancient trees, we have created
home for nomad and immigrant
a heart for a family.

Retirement. Rewirement. Realignment.

Ingrid Frengley-Vaipuna

It has to be done. I am done.

40 years is enough.

I do not want to grow old carrying

young people's trauma, rudeness, violence, depression, sadness

desperately presenting them with alternatives

they ignore or denigrate

or, just occasionally enough to have kept me here,

understand, visualise, internalise, and fly!

Waitonga Day
Ingrid Frengley-Vaipuna

On Waitangi Day at our place in Pātea

we host Waitonga Day

Taranaki Tongan families come to swim and talk and feast

younger ones, taller and bigger than most,

wander off to Pae Pae while

the sullen pig turns watched by men who

laugh as only Tongans can.

Later, after feasting, bellies full of pork and beer and 'ofa

they sing wholeheartedly.

Turbine Haiku
Ingrid Frengley-Vaipuna

the windmills can stay

serenely rotating arms

wafting peace my way

The University of Pātea

Trevor M. Landers

I look at the youth
on
the streets
      and
         s
           e
            e
              potential
                    l
                    o
                    o
                    k
                    i
                    n
                    g

              for

                    o p p o r t u n i t y,

I
  see
     rangatahi
         in

a

world of uber-fast complexification

turning

in

to

soft young males

and

soft young females

h |a | r |d |e |n |e d

by

attitudes of circumscription that we, sanctimonious adults

harbour, like we were never young

or did not make mistakes ourselves.

The human condition is:

trial and error, exasperation, resilience then.... mastery

Know them before you judge them

They are you, and you were them.

So now you know:

Egmont St is the visceral University of Pātea.

Faculty of Medical Sciences at Ngāti Ruanui Health;

Faculty of Animal Health at Taranaki Veterinary Centre;

Faculty of Māori Studies at the Aotea Waka;

Faculty of Arts and Social Science at Aotea Utanganui;

Annexes of the Faculty of Fine Arts at the Bank Room & PG;

Faculty of Gastronomy at Four Square Pātea and three cafés

The streets are lecture theatres.

keep all ambitions & aspirations alive!

taku mounga
Vaughan Rapatahana

[Hokia ki tō maunga kia purea ai koe e ngā hau a Tāwhirimātea]

Ki te ngau ai te āwangawnga
me hoki ahau
ki taku mounga

Taranaki
i ngā wāhi katoa
ka kurehu ki te hukarere
ko te kaitiaki mārohirohi
mō te katoa i tēnei wāhi,
      me
aua hau o te uru, hohoro ana
whiua atu ngā here
mō āke tonu atu.

tēnei wāhi tapu he oranga ngākau
he rite tonu ki te whakakitenga
ka whakapaia i ahau,
ia wā
ka karanga mai kia hoki mai

hei tāmata ake
i ahau anō.

[my mountain
[Return to your mountain, so that you can be cleansed by the
winds of Tawhirimatea.]

whenever the angst bites
I must return
to my mountain.
Taranaki,
omnipresent
looms niveous,
the majestic guardian
of all nearby,
       &
those swift west winds
whisk away the claustral
once and for all.

this sanctuary of solace
is epiphanic,
it catharsises me,
each time
I am called back
to reclaim myself.]

Pātea: mano whenua

nā Trevor M. Landers

Pātea :: mano whenua
    kia kāeaea ia ki mauī, ki matau
    ka kite ia i tōna kuia, ka pupū ake te matemate-ā-one ki
tana ūkaipō
    ko te wahi whakahirahira
tikanga-ā-iwi, ko te whanga o Turi,
  o Māui poutūmārō hoki,
    i puta nei hei kaiwhakatū, hei kaiwhakangahau
      I tōna wā ka tū ko ia hei rangatira mō te rohe nei i te tau
1983, te tīmatatanga o te tautitotito o te waiata rongonui ko:
        Poi E.

He rahi ake tēnei taone ki tērā
    He nui ake i te kāri, te haerenga mai rānei a Paul Holmes i
ngā rā o mua
    He nui ake i te katinga mai o te wheketere
        mīti i te tau 1982
            kei konei te panapana
  o te manawa,

ahurea me te hāpori
Kia ai te tangata karu tore,
'he kanohi hōmiromiro'
pēnei i te pūpū atamarama e whiti ana
i roto i te ahoroa.

Ko Pātea, Ka whakapōkaikaha i au

Trevor M. Landers

Ko Pātea, ka whakapōkaikaha i au

    he nui ake i te rongorongo mātua

    te waiata nama rongonui

    te whare whakamātao mīti tāwhito rānei

kei kōnei ngā kōrero e ora ana,

    ka noho ngā tāngata ki aua kōrero

    he akonga hōu tāku, ia te wā hoki ai ki a koe

Te hokinga mai a Parihaka

Vaughan Rapatahana

i hoki
        ki raro
ki Parihaka
i tērā wiki.

i hiahiatia e ahau.
        he iti noa hei tūtei
        mēnā he tūruhi koe
kōpipiri ana ki rō he wakanoho,
        he rōpū kaihekengaru pōrohe
        e ngaro ana rānei
        ki runga i tētehi whakatakanga
kūnakunaku nui
ngaru tino momoho.

kua w h a k a n u i a te urupā,
ko taua whakamaharatanga
 e whakaora ana
i a Te Whiti
kua riro atu ki te māwhe,
me ētahi o ngā whare
kua rurerure ki ngā riwha hōu.
            he marino tonu te wairua,
he māhaki tonu ngā tāngata o tēnei rohe,

ahakoa te mamae o te hītori.

erangi
he ārai
anahe ēnei

i roto i te ariari marino nei
he awenga tūturu
ā, ahakoa he kawa te rongo,
ko rongo ahau i te hira.

ko Parihaka
horahia ana te w h a k a h i r a h i r a,
ko tōna tūnga monoa,
me whakarongona te reka
e tātou katoa.

[Parihaka return

went back
            down
to Parihaka
last week.

I needed to.

there is not much to sleuth
if you are tourists
sardined in a campervan,

or a scruff of lost surfers
on a misdirected
bonanza wave
extravaganza.

the urupā has e x p a n d e d,
that obelisk
immortalising Te Whiti
has become more achromatic,
and some buildings
brandish new scars.
the atmosphere remains peaceful,
the people of this district ever humble,
despite the agony of history.

but
these are merely
camouflage.

inside this palpable stillness
there is tangible presence.
and while the tang is tart,
I taste the epochal.

Parihaka
is sumptuous s p r e a d,
its estimable standing,
something we all should savour.]

The day Albi and the Wolves played the Kākāramea Hall

Te Aniwā Braddock

'Albi and the Wolves', © Te Aniwā Braddock, 2022

I am not sure
how I saw this advertised
Albi and the Wolves
passing through Kākāramea
like a band of wandering troubadours
sowing the gospel
of foot-tapping alt-folk.

We turn up
just before commencement at 7
as if we have wandered into
an extraordinary meeting
of Greypower, waiting for....
the music interlude.
This is not a jibe
or an intended as an insult
merely a commentary
on gig demographics tonight.

It is good toe tapping fun
if only the talkers near the bar
would shut up and let those
who have come to listen, listen.
At the end, he buys me
a commemorative t-shirt &
clutching merch and memories in hand
we turn and head toward Ōpunakē.

South Taranaki mourning

Mikaela Nyman

October 2021

Hard to fathom that it was born to be buoyant this
sleek body now flabby
still juvenile yet undeniably female

Buoyancy is an upward force, a rush of laughter,
an upthrust of molecules saluting the sky –
but can you ever trust your body?

That photo, was I the only one to see freshly tilled
soil, undulating land, grooves strangely square?
So often desire blurs the clarity of vision

Named Te Karu o Kōteoteo – the eye of the Kōteoteo awa –
a riverine eye no larger in size than a cow's

An eye offered back to Tangaroa, guardian of the ocean,
once the naming ceremony was over

Foraging peacefully off the South Taranaki Bight
then bam – dorsal fin, baleen, fluke carried ashore.
But why?

At only 24, Te Karu o Kōteoteo was lovingly disassembled
buried in an ancient practice carried out by several iwi.
A rāhui in place from Ōtahi river to Waiwiri

Our children used to climb through a model
of a blue whale heart the size of a red bumper car
at Te Papa

Meanwhile, the Department of Conservation collects samples
of blubber to better understand
Te Karu o Kōteoteo's whakapapa, the ocean's health

the impact of a lifetime, pools
of pollutants accumulated

Hei maumahara: Clarrie Zimmerman
Trevor M Landers

Finding a secret path off Powerhouse Rd, the Kōtare tipped waves not blue, azure, or ultramarine, but finest royal blue. Not for QEII today, but Clarrie, a beachcomber, fisherman *par excellence*; some would say an eremite, a solitarian, a loner. But Clarrie was a kind, thoughtful man, indulgent to a small Kaupokonui boy; never brusque or terse, but it is true that one learnt breviloquence in his orbit---the eyes seem to say: enough talking. Yes. If heaven exists, Clarrie is there, fishing the coast.

Te Pou a Turi me ngā pūrehu kapohau ki Waipipi

Nā Trevor M. Landers

       Koinei te wāhi
kōnei
ko te kaihautū a Turi
nāna i mauria mai te waka o Aotea
ū mai ki uta

ngā kainga
ngā māra
ka timata i muri tata mai.

Kua huri te ao hurihuri
kua pahemo ngā rautau
ko te ahi kā
ko te muru raupatu
ko ngā whakataunga tiriti
inaiānei, he mārama ake te heke mai.

Patohia ki tawhiti
ngā pūrehu kapohau
tohu o te ata hou
he ōhanga pātītī me te miraka
inaiānei kua tata kākāriki
me te tino kākāriki tonu
i te wā kei te heke mai.

Unzipping in the Pātea River

Katherine Joyce

Will you
unzip me slowly?

Savour the release
of the words.
    confessions....
        transgressions.

When you Unzip me...
will I pour out
all those thoughts?
Will they come out
like a wave...
or like little drip drip
of a shower having already passed.

But don't stop there.
I'm feeling the zipper of my soul go...
click clack.... it's tickling....
caressing the soft flesh and
hidden scars.

Unzip me slowly...

so I can step out.

Step out of this old, pretty dress.

Let it fall to the sand.

Let these old thoughts and fears

lay discarded...

ok

kicked away.

Unzip me slowly...

....will you?

To those who let go
Michaela Stoneman

Again, the fantails tried to get in
through the top sash windows
I think their primary motive is
to summon certain death
or devour the late summer flies

Our sky is jam-packed
clusterfucks of stars
twinkling their butts off
midnight flashers
reveal all for just a split second

Thrills tasted
space dust congregates
in dual corners
where our lips meet
sherbet inhaled
Eating chalk and glitter

Droplets of rain fall on me
just the same as everyone else
please do not judge me
for being flippant
I am easily amused
I live in a small town

Please visit me at six o'clock
when the wind drops so we can
hear each other speak
Whispering forgotten chants
chanting forgotten whispers
making up things
to become tomorrow's lies

Feelings of loss are granted
to those who let go.

Imagining Pātea from El Salvador

Roselina Cook

Editor, this is too hard!

The people will laugh!

When I conjured the word Pātea, sight unseen

I thought of a cuddle, and then paté

So perhaps a picnic blanket on a sunny afternoon

And a place I can now point to on a map of New Zealand[11]

---

[11] TRANSLATION from Spanish by Trevor M. Landers: Imaginando Patea de El Salvador. ¡Editura, esto es demasiado difícil!/¡La gente se reirá!/Cuando conjuré Patea, vista invisible/ Pensé en un abrazo, y luego paté/Así que tal vez una manta de picnic en una tarde soleada/Y un lugar que ahora puedo señalar en un mapa de Nueva Zelanda.

Leaving the Old Pātea Hospital

Mac Dempsey

The old fabric curtains round the bed are blue and tatty.
The corridor is warm and the whole place smells of antiseptic.
I am cradled into you, asleep as you sip the glass of water.
I feel your arms enveloping me. They are heavy and warm.
When the nurse places me in the cot there is a warm shape
of me on your body. When you hold me, you hold me loose,
uncertain what your arms may do to a new-born. You speak in
repetitions, like a gospel singer with a voice as languid as water,
smooth and quenching somehow. My skin feels rigid, like the
leather of a traditional kayak, I gurgle at your sleepy blue-sky
smiles. You want to bath me. You lie me underwater, and tell
me what a good boy I am. More ecstatic gurgling. I still love
the water. You raise exhausted arms at my triumph. After four
days your Dr and Matron tell you can take me home. It is then
I meet Dad. He googles at me, and I gurgle back in a more or
less appreciative manner. He holds me. His hands are rough
and worn. Later, I discover he is a farmer. Once at home on
the farm, I discover I am not an only child. I miss the smell of
cleanliness and military hygiene. I miss the bright, powerful
lights which take a few seconds to warm up and reach "full
beam". I miss the cubicle divider and our enforced afternoon
rests. Most of all, I am proud of what my birth certificate says:
Born in Pātea.

The Place where my mother was born
Makayla Wood

We return to the town where my mother was born. This is my first time here. We drive past her old house, and the old hospital where she was born. It is derelict and we both feel sad. Mum goes silent. She does not like the look of this abandoned building. It looks like a wrecking ball has exploded just where the mothers and their babies used to be. Sometimes looking back is painful. Like now.

Pillar of Hope

eRiQ Quaadgras

No matter

how down

you might get

there will always

be some loving lifeline

out there in the world

just send a sign, just shake a tree

just reach out and share – even with me

the troubles that could cloud your mind

there are those that

truly

can be kind.[12]

---

[12] The first two poems on the page appeared in Crisp, Vol.2, (May June 2021).

Never Give Up

Justine Joyce Dreyer

It is ok to back away

It's ok to hold your words

It's ok to ask people not to disturb you

When you are feeling down

Never give up.

Just never give up!

It's ok to be brave

It's also ok if you are not feeling

It's ok to shy away

Never give up.

Just never give up!

Storms

eRiQ Quaadgras

A storm is brewing

the world is a whirly cauldron

which crafty creation

can wither the weather

when darkness prevails

upon us all

outside the skies

are turning black

inside our souls

are fighting back

against the power

of the cloud.[13]

---

[13] This poem appeared in Crisp, Vol.3, (2021).

Unarticulated, Undiminished (Pātea Habour)

Te Tuhi Holdsworthy and Trevor M. Landers

I cannot touch her, so light with oblivion

the way she steps into first light, the

sea off Pātea; you can hear it seize her

the throaty growling of volcanic stones

slowly manufacturing sand with every tidal pull

she slipped away long before I found the words for it.

We throw water after those who leave us,

may it not dry before you return –

 a woman is like the sea,

deft scent of ozone, the sweet waters of Turi.

Dream-River

Trevor M Landers

ethereal

astonishing beauty

evoked through rapturous lensing,

swooping and gliding down rushing over stones

descending into your abyssal canyons

alongside schools of startled fish,

I wish I was a frigate bird

witnessing from above the uncanny patterns

the waterways carve through the landscape.

a reaffirmation of the beauty of you, river,

and an urgent call to protect you

mainly, from all humankind.[14]

---

[14] First published in the May 2022 issue of Tarot.

Pātea perambulation, 2022

Volodymyr Shevchenko

Passing through; stoppage, ice-creams or irritable bowel
kick a can of L&P down the Main St, listen for echoes,
walking beneath the Aotea Canoe, landed here after a pit stop
at Kaupokonui, Trevor says. Walk back through the faded
kōrero of museum history: Aotea Utanganui, out onto the
bright street tweeting inside the belly of the great Tutunui.
Kia ora Pātea.

The Pātea River

Jax Stephens

Calming friend

grass as green as a wet painting

all heavy emotions dissipated

in the daily burble of water

Pātea sun-river, you are my sanctuary

the buddy who never judges me

just going with the flow.

The Beach at Pātea

Ruhansi Amarasinghe and Ashlee Hutton

I stand at the line where blue and brown collide.
I embrace this bickering marriage
waves arguing spume-tipped points
earth's crust resisting obstinately.

I look to my left and spot a small fishing vessel
leaving the dock, crashing against rough seas.
The pier at one end of the beach detonates wave explosions
They crash against the rocks with unpredictability.

Gentler blue waves crash over my feet
igniting shivers down my body every time.
rays of sunlight project themselves onto the water
glistening like precious jewels.

Fishing off the coast of Pātea
David Denning

Now I understand with fresh prescience

the shipping forecasts on National Radio

a spiteful wind has kicked up bilious from nowhere

the swell information has commandeered my stomach

we are bobbing around in the South Taranaki Bight

like a cork in a jeroboam of champagne at a wedding.

All thoughts of actual fishing scuppered

the ominous cracking storm breaking over us

a bit of late afternoon pyrotechnics

to bring into sharp relief, my land-lubbers waltz

but in the ice-laden bin fresh Tarakihi and Warehou lie

looking back at me with dull and squeamish eyes

interrogating my enfeebled disposition as if to say:

Really? Is this what you do for fun?

A Parishioner of St. Georges, Pātea

Anonymous

The card pulled from the deck claims
    you stand at an impasse.
        Branches overlapping at awkward angles,
    the town cleansed with rain
  bristle at the obvious metaphor
    or admire the architecture.
Back inside, by the fire,
    the heat desiccates your eyes
        nourishes the imagery of suffering.
Take this and eat it, the Lord said.
   Symbolism only gets you so far
You often feel the urge to turn here
   Orange glow in the corrugation of an ear
a hymn sung to the limits of their ranges
   like an octopus caught in brackish waters
     a lot of thrashing around until next week, anyway.

The call

Tony Beyer

my neighbour Ray
enumerates his
favourite activities

as fishin'
huntin'
and whitebaitin'

as well as stayin'
at his mate's
son-in-law's sheep farm

out the back of Manga'
where even if they
catch or kill or net nothin'

they always
have a lot
of laughs

and though it sounds
bestial and I know
I'd be useless

I want to say to him
next time
take me

Eeling in the Upper Whenuakura

Hōhepa Kumeroa

Āe, if you want the fat

Grand-daddy ones

paddle up the river

find some over-hanging willow

put white bread

in your Agee® jar

and stand poised with

the gaff, son: oh, happy days!

The Staunch as Women at the Pātea Pool

Pania Liddell

She's not here for vengeance
despite the bluster
and brooding body language---
Actually, she's quite calm.
The drama is over
no-one is bombing
no watery explosions at the shallow end.
I guess many have tried
to burn her before ---no running!---
her nerves knew the shock of accusation
and full-on verbal assaults
she is impervious to rude language
or daggered thoughts
even after giving a growling
but she is not resentful.
just doing her job
but she could smile more.
Maybe hire a swanky PR firm
get on the socials, bae, glam you up!
Soften the exterior
less of the *Game of Thrones* face
more *Downtown Abbey* vibes
These scallywags will grow to be villagers
with nervous hearts not violent hands
and they will learn
to outfox the women they can't yet burn,
yeah, the staunch as woman at the pool
'Shot, Miss!'

Pātea perambulation 1984
Vaughan Rapatahana

corralled inside a Clarendon catacomb,
& after sluicing an ale or two
                                too many,
fleeing flailing Fijian farmhand fists,
I hitchiked north west
                        the next morning.

no seasonal
worker
but relation-
ship shirker.

I'd abandoned my mark IV –
            purchased copacetic in Kaikohe
                                aeons ago
                                for a few hundred
                                and a stash of hash –
a behemoth rammed hard
against a clay bank,
askew a shingle rut
up a mislaid valley
in another motu.
                        the frayed dice swaying
                        like boozed propellors.
deserted my Ngāpuhi whānau
& in fugue state meltdown

flown waveringly
to bother my brother -

                    some sort of milk factory boffin -

in the guts of Waverley.
next loomed Pātea,
my own tūrangawaewae.

                  I'd slithered into
              the maternity annex

decades before,
while my father had a tutū

             at the meatworks.

the town was already shrivelled,
when, squatting cateleptic adrift

           a fading dairy -
           my thumb doing the walking
           moody showers ever stalking -

from nowhere in particular,
in faint flux of hope,
I dredged up
a dream dyad –

Poi E, e awhi mai ra,
wondering where
Dalvanius

      was

         right

           then.[15]

---

[15] First published in Mātātuhi Taranaki: A bilingual journal of literature, Vol.2, no.1, (February 2022), at www.matatuhitaranaki.ac.nz

Pakakohi Chicaneries

Pania Liddell

Donald McLean
    speaks with a serpentine tongue:
        'Just give us the land
        & we won't have to steal it
      by administrative fiat, legal fictions
        or other disingenuous means'.
Mokoia, Tamahere,
      Taumaha, Tangahoe and Pakakohi
      are the names of crimes committed
        entreaties broken
    of promises made and wilfully undelivered
      Pātea, Weraroa, and Waitōtara too.
Everyone knows, the disgraced Native Minister
    ministers not for Māori
      but for land-hunger and his pecuniary advantage
    now he lies besmirched in an earthen grave
      the judgments of history
        these are your penitentiary, Sir,
    the day of reckoning draws ever nearer.

Stereotypical Māori

For My Wairua

The captivating Māori
The waiata Māori
The Louis Vuitton Māori

The 'smart for a' Māori
The mean Māori (mean) Māori
The Police 10/7 Māori

The 'don't speak te reo' Māori
The 'never grew up on the marae' Māori
The 'who do you come from' Māori
The blood quantum Māori
The 1 / 4 Māori
The sign along the dotted line Māori

The uprising of Māori
The resilience of Māori
The brilliance of Māori

Typhoon Phillips
Anonymous

A demon off twenty paces
frighteningly quick on his day
     damn near unplayable on a seaming day
     uncomfortable on uncovered grass wickets
Like any belligerent paceman
an unexpected bouncer is a lethal weapon
     Flowing blonde locks blown in the breeze
     another unsuspecting batter dances the two-step
"Brucie, Brucie" some wags on the boundary chant
willing the Taranaki quick to snare another victim for Pātea.

He aihikirimi i Pātea

Nā Trevor M. Landers

Ka tū mātou,

i te nuinga o te wā, ki te Rutaka Runga

He aha tō tino reka?

Rōpere? Tiakarete? Kapia pai-pai?

He tikanga tuku iho inaiānei.[16]

---

[16] ICE-CREAM IN PATEA. We always stop/usually at the Top Dairy/What is your favourite flavour?/Strawberry? Chocolate? Goody-goody gum drop?/It is a tradition now.

Winter Sports

Denzel Adlam

My bones still clicking into place
the sun is starting to arc over the horizon
arctic type air pushing through my lungs
"Boys, this is it", said with frost-breath leaving the mouth.
All the brothers' heads down in silence, not a soul to be heard
Mātua breaks the silence with a deep breath
We all look up, there is a slight whisper: 'This is it"
he looks at us, a bloodthirst in his gaze.
His teeth grinding like a saw cutting metal
his palms fully clenched, grabbing at the air.

With every brother "stripped" in a numbered jersey
we take the leap from locker room to field
passing through a dark, gloomy corridor
our pupils struggle to adjust to the light shining through
our minds set to the field of battle
I feel a slight breeze across my body like a sea current
I restrain my conscience: we are on the field.

Our boots pound into thick mud

our bodies warming up for the game like a winter heater

the grass underfoot is a thick cake of mud

consuming our sprigs as we run.

The sun shines shyly but we do not feel it.

Our hands are so numb we cannot feel the pressure of the ball

as it passes through our hands one by one.

With the first blast of the whistle we all come together

gathered around in a circular shape: "This is it"

repeated in a craven manner, with every single brother

wrapped around another, we are all in for the last call:

"Tūturu whakamaua, kia tina!

Tina!

Haumi ē!

Hui ē!

Tāiki ē!"

The sound of the whistle bursts in our ears.[17]

---

[17] A version of this poem entitled 'A Cold Winter's Day' was highly commended in the 2017 Ronald Hugh Morrieson Literary Awards.

Poi E Won't Break Your Heart

Airana Ngarewa

My whānau are not a front row whānau
Never have been.
Koko's kids were out of town
When those waiata were composed –
Chasing high school certificates
At fancy boarding schools.
Everybody else got in on it
Paid their dues
Were dragged along to every practice
Were cussed out and made to do it right
Perfect.
The lyrics are in their genes now
Been with them longer than their lovers
Will stay with them too –
You can't divorce Poi E
Break up with Aku Raukura
Cheat on Ngoi Ngoi.
Taranaki will one day erupt out of existence
Whenuakura dry up
Aotea disappears into the earth
And Pātea Māori Club will remain –

The same whānau singing
the same lyrics
to the same beat of the poi.
Nothing is forever
Except the PMC.
The whole earth could up and disappear
and you'd still hear the uncles sing:
'Ka tipu te pono'
And the aunties sing:
'Me te tika'
and you'd still see my whānau in the third row
getting the actions wrong.

Poi E me Paraoa

Name Withheld

Tōku hoa aroha

i mua i tōku matenga

kaua e waiho noa i āhau

whakatangihia a Poi E, ā, mauria mai he paraoa māku

Kia hākoakoa ahau i a au e mawehe atu i tēnei ao

murua mai i āhau e kare

he pai ake i te rekareka.[18]

---

[18] ENGLISH TRANSLATION: My darling/before I die/don't leave me alone/ play Poi E and fetch me some Paraoa/Let me slip away from this realm in a very happy state/forgive me dear, it is better than an orgasm! (Trevor M. Landers, September 2022).

Another Day at the Office

Rachael Kellogg

Big sky tractors

sweep over the rugged greens

to furrow

rounded mounds

of aching browns

just warming up

to the precious diesel music

of a newly sunburnt Saturday.[19]

---

[19] This poem was very highly commended in the open poetry section of the 2013 Ronald Hugh Morrieson Literary Awards.

Nō hea koe?

Gareth Aston Carwyn Kahui

Ko 'Egmont hardcore' te maunga

Ko most polluted (by nutrient standard levels) river in NZ te awa

Ko 91 Mitsubishi Lancer SX saloon, reg'd & warranted te waka

Ko Social Sciences, Westpac, WINZ, The Local, me Pak N Save nga iwi

Ko te hill me Kaitoke Prison ngā hapu

Ko. www te Rangatira

Ko 'doing shopping'te marae

Ko blankets me composure ōku Tūpuna

Ko channel 1, 2 & 3 ōku Mātua

Kei te 'bearnt place' e noho ana

Ko indegenous tāku ingoa[20]

---

[20] This poem was achieved a 3rd placing in the open poetry section of the 2012 Ronald Hugh Morrieson Literary Awards.

The Freezing Works Virgin
Name Withheld

You came like a fur-seal

rippling the water and slithering over rocks

into the decrepit ruins of the factory

primal and eager

I drew closer; you laid me down

I watched the shadows on the walls

looming large

I waited for the earth to tremble

but all I heard was the distant groan

of the ocean.

His Highness (Little black shag)

Elvisa van der Leden

Feathers so black

with that slick sheen

between each catch

you thoughtfully preen

Oh, how proud

a stance you hold

puffed out breast

ever so bold

With sharpened eyes

you spot your pray

depart the perch

plunge into the bay

Inspiring technique

you glide through the deep

a small herring

betwixt your beak

Royal you are
in your fishy realm
while numbers of
peasant gulls overwhelm

A fisherman king
on his throne of rock
a strong independent
estranged from the flock

While small in stature
with grace and beauty
such virtue imprinted
upon pure scenery

Falling towards Kākāramea

Anonymous

This name is on my tongue, the place I first felt the feverish

F

A

L

L

I

N

G

I'm still learning to fly, falling to earth like a parachutist.

'Ofa anga

Ingrid Frengley-Vaipuna

In our kitchen

the smell of boiled fish heads

and a pile of sucked naked bones.

You're home

I go looking for your solidity

and the orange dog

who follows you everywhere.[21]

---

[21] This poem was highly commended in the 2014 Ronald Hugh Morrieson Literary Awards.

Gladstone Road

Jason Wright

That way lies Gladstone Road
clothed in Douglas Fir
wildfires, home-cooked food
and us, brother.

Arriving year one by motorbike
year two by Austin Allegro
bright as the sun
battling rutted gravel roads
lumpy river stones
turning upon a rise with hard men
and their Land Rovers

Under our tent fly
its poles lost on the highway
we kick off clinging clothes
boots and darned Norsewear socks
blue and red from the bargain bin
and hang them on the line
the way Dad did

The fire; crackling, sparking
to see that sideways stinging rain
that soaked us to the bone
out on Gladstone Road.[22]

---

[22] This poem was placed 2nd in the Open Poetry section in the 2014 Ronald Hugh Morrieson Literary Awards.

Aotea Utanganui : The Museum of South Taranaki

Katherine Joyce and Trevor M. Landers

We love museums

repositories of knowledge

and curiosity

fusty cabinets,

slick dioramas,

yellowy photographs:

We will take them all.

Recently, to our wonderment and surprise

the ghost town of Richardson,

present day Ngutuwera

was surveyed in 1898 by de Dennis Fraser

aided and abetted by a future Secretary of Labour

Edward Tregear, him of *The Aryan Māori* fame

which seemed wishful thinking then and now

but the Vedic and Sanskrit origins----

anyway, on March 1893,

183 sections

on prime confiscated Ngā Rauru Kiitahi land

went under the auctioneer's hammer

though only a handful sold

eventually all would become paddocks

critics lambasted the idea

as patently absurd

as unsuited for a settlement

as ridiculous

as many contemporaries

could imagine

it just goes to show

some people

are wickedly imaginative

and follies like this

lurk in museums.

My friends
Raian Lal:

My friends are all stupid
but I'm not immune
at least I don't eat worms
or get arrested.

Playing with my friends
I play to their annoyance,
I play too but they still get grumpy
that is the way it is with friends.

My friends I have gone places
I have travelled with the thieves,
but why did I help them
steel some cheese?

My friends that give money
The ones who get yelled at
The ones that stand and fight
While I stand there and watch.

I love them all.

The Top Dairy

Rosanne Oakes

The Top Dairy has always been there

but to me it was Jeffs' – the family, not a man

It was their home out the back

where my youngest brother got a spin in their washing machine

courtesy of the mischievous older boys.

Then it was all lollies and ice cream.

Now it is a truck driver's breakfast, lunch and dinner,

chicken and chips washed down with something fizz,

a pie for breakfast on the way to school,

another big bottle of coloured fizz on the way home,

and back again for a white loaf and a paper wrapped parcel

I wonder if they call them chip butties? Sociological research.

Notably generous ice creams for travellers and beach goers

provides an easy greasy feed after a day on the golf course.

A Friday night, well actually a nightly fav,

judging from the cars lined up, fish and chips flowing.

Yes, the Top Dairy has always been there.

Redefining Pātea

Joseph Kalisa

Possible meanings:

1. verb: To give someone or to ask someone something.

> *e.g., He always wanted to pātea his mother a cow as a gift.*

2. noun, referring to a hot drink:

> *e.g., Can you pass me that pātea, it's cold outta here.*

3. Noun describing a good person.

> *e.g., Pātea is a very beautiful person, and everyone loves being in their company.*

4. Verb. Resistance to poor treatment

> *e.g., Their community has pātea'd all these years from the confrontations of their inconsiderate neighbours.*

You can be anything you want to be, Pātea!

Redefining Pātea Again

Cristina & Mugurel Tudor

1. ['pə tɪə/] noun, fem., the fifth-born royal princess in Slavic Baltic countries. From pętь, five.
2. [pə 'teːə/] noun, plural form of pateus, liver pie baked in the Roman Empire as funeral wake food. From παστός (pastós).
3. [pə 'teːə/] noun, horizontal stone structure at the bottom of a door, found in medieval Scandinavian farmhouses, used to vigorously stomp the mud off the wooden clogs. From plættan,to smack.
4. [pə 'tiː/] noun, the orange-yellowy colour of papaya tea.
5. ['pʌ teːə/] noun, any of the registered IKEA patents, short from Swedish *uppfinningsårbetäpatentikea*, a crazy invention patented by IKEA.[23]

---

[23] EDITOR'S NOTE: We asked a Rwandan, a Romanian and a Finn to re-define meanings of the word, Pātea, without googling the term, safe in the knowledge the word was unfamiliar to both. The exercise was designed to show that meaning is largely constructed and we can choose the narratives we want to focus on and reject those that do not serve us beneficially. We are constructions, and although we face constraints, we don't have to accept the constrictures they impose. With hard work, determination, support, and positivity the limits of our achievement are largely self-imposed. Again, we do not diminish the repercussions of structural oppression but encourage readers to find ways to resist and find methods of self-empowerment.

Haihana Ngāwakataurua Te Tahua Pehimana
Nā Trevor M. Landers

He tama rangatira nō Pātea
ka tukuna atu ki te pakanga tuatahi o te ao
me Te Hokowhitu a Tū
ka whakatau ai i Melita
i mua i te whawhai ki Tākei
he rongonui mō te haka o te ope o Tū
i mua i te whakaekenga o te puke 791
ka tāwhangawhanga ki te whawhai
korekau he take kōnatunatu
ka taotū ki runga o Chunuk Bair
katahi ka eke i te kaipuke hōhipera
ki Suvla Bay
ka hoki mai anō ki Taranaki
i reira whakatū ai e tōna Whaea, he whakahari nui rawa
ka tae atu e te Koromatua, kōrerotia ai
erangi rā ko te mea pouri ko tērā,
tekau mā tahi ngā rā mai tōna hokinga mai
ka mate tēnei toa pakanga
te tama toa o Pātea
nā te momia o te urutā rewharewha

Broad translation:

Sargeant Ngāwakataurua Te Tahua Pehimana

Proud son of Pātea

went away to the First World War

with the First Māori Contingent

resting in Malta, before fighting in Turkey

famous for the contigent haka

being storming up Hill 791

dashing headlong into the fight unflinchingly

no quandaries at all

later, he was wounded on Chunuk Bair

evacuated to a hospital ship in Suvla Bay

he returns to Taranaki

where his mother throws him a massive party

the mayor attends and speaks

and then, a time of great sadness

11 days after returning

Pātea's warrior son

loses his last battle

the kiss of the Influenza Epidemic.

Pātea's River Queen

Te Tuhi Holdsworthy

1.

Purveyor of the trite, stater of the obvious
just sit your wondrous black ass down here,
so, we sit on the kerb, in front of the Museum,
exchanging air, wistful glances. 'You are a one'
I think, necking a beer.

2.

'Oh Pleez!' she says, clutching her bottle of
cider: sensing invisible scorn-- she mutters on,
glaring at her feet the veins almost luminescent under
diaphanous skin. My mind conjures river water,
us as picaresque kids under the bridge.

3.

The grass-lined banks of the river, squeaking
& skinny-dipping for hours throwing stones at gulls
attracted by rich offal lying under the sun as
the august Māori King & radiant Māori Queen pass.

But you were a wildcat, you never offered a kiss

but you teased us all during that long, sultry

summer: and we loved you even more for it.

4.

Let's not sup melancholy, each other's blocked-up

nostalgia for distant loves that were better as apparitions

than realities anyways. I'm sure of it. There is a ghostly moon

over Pātea tonight; the kēhua are out. You say you hate this

place but now I know you are drunk. I admire your feet.

5.

As she says it, she knows she is beautiful. The net

of stars over Victoria St are uncommonly bright,

as if politely asking the streetlights to have the

night off. We walk back through town, resisting

the tyranny of memory. "I love you man' she

says finally, near her Mum's whare: "I love you too, Sissy" I say,

knowing this will all be lost when the perditions

of morning arrive with solemn familiarity.

Te ora a taiohi

Name Withheld

He uaua te taiohitanga
Te pēhinga ki te mahi i tēnā
Te pēhinga ki te mahi i tēnei

Ehara āhau i te akonga mōhio
Ehara āhau i te toa hākinakinaa
Ehara āhau i te ringa toi
Ka whakapau kaha āhau

Karekau he wāhitau rerehua
Kare rawa tō mātou whare e kitea i roto i te maheni
Ko mātou ngā morehu
Ko mātou te hunga kua wareware tia
Ko mātou ngā tatauranga wahangū

I etahi wā ka rongo āhau i ngā reo
Ngā reo mai i te moana
Ngā reo nō te urupā
He reo mō te pai, he reo mō te kino
Ngā reo wairua mai i ō mātou tūpuna

He toropuku tāku

tē taea te whakapuaki

I a au e tamaiti ana

I whakapākeke ake i mua i tāku wā

Ka mau āhau i tēnei mea ngaro anā he patunga tapu

Ka kawea āhau i te hara me te wahangū.[24]

---

[24] TRANSLATION: Being young can be difficult/pressure to do that/ pressure to do this/ I am not a gifted student/ I am not good at sports/I am not artistic/I do my best/I don't have a fancy address/our house will never be in any magazine/ we are survivors/ we are the forgotten/ we are the silent statistic/ Sometimes I hear voices/voices from the sea/voices from the grave/voices for good, and voices for evil/ghostly voices from our ancestors/I have a secret I cannot utter/ I was a child made adult before my time/I carry a crime in silence.

Kaua e mataku ki ngā rangatahi o ēnei rā

Anonymous

Lenticular clouds, South Taranaki, ©Trevor M Landers August 2022

E mōhio ana koutou i hē hoki mātou

Ka nui ake ā mātou hapa; whakahara atu!

Ētehi wā, ka hinga kia ako

Ka inu waipiro mātou, ka moepuku, ka momi, ka takahi ture

Erangi ka ora tonu mātou.

Tono mai mō te āwhina. I rite au ki a koe i mua rānō. [25]

---

[25] TRANSLATION: Don't Fear the Youth of Today. Fear not youth of today/ You know we got it wrong too/We mad huge mistakes; mammoth!/ We lived and learned sometimes/We drank, we copulated, we smoked, we broke the law but we survived/Reach out for help/I was once like you.

Kapua ki runga o Pātea

Tamszyn Broughton & Trevor M. Landers

He pai ki āhau ngā āhuareka ngāwari
i ētehi wā i te wā e hikoi ana ki te kāinga mai i te kura
He pai ki āhau te takoto ki waenganui i te papa whutupōro
me te matakitaki i ngā kapua

He pai ki a au te titiro whakamiha
ki ngā momo kapua katoa o te rangi.
He rerekē ngā āhua, rerekē te rahi, rerekē ngā tae
Kua kanikani puta noa i te rangi

He pai ki āhau te piki teitei
e whakaaro ana āhau ki runga i te rangi
e huri haere ana puta noa i Pātea
me te kore i te āwangawanga o te ao

Kāore te mahi-a-kura a ngā kapua
Kāore te whakawā a ngā kapua
Ka tata tonu mai ngā kapua

Ko ngā kapua ka whakamarie i au.[26]

---

[26] TRANSLATION: Clouds over Pātea. I like simple pleasures/sometimes while walking home from school/I like to lie down in the middle of the rugby ground/ and watch the clouds. I like to gaze up in awe/ at all the different types of cloud in the sky. Different shapes, difference sizes, different colours/dancing across the sky. I like to climb high, my thinking up in the sky/rolling across Pātea/without any worldly anxieties. Clouds do no schoolwork/clouds make no judgments/the clouds are always near to us/the clouds comfort me.

Heading North to Manaia

Trevor M. Landers

Heading North to Manaia, Source: Trevor M. Landers

A familiar hikoi

a pilgrimage often made

from Ngaio to Manaia.

The sloping right hander over the Pātea River

a territorial signal arrival beckons a little closer

the old Freezing Works frozen on the wharf.

In the twilight of daylight savings, if you are peckish
perhaps stop briefly for an indulgent ice-cream cone
Raspberry or Strawberry; thanks, Pavlov's dog.

Take a moment to savour creamy goodness
in the glint of the sun, Mounga Taranaki resolute
there is a radial compass to guide us in.

a heartland, Rauru and Ruanui country through here
the roads serpentine, just like the rivers
Leaving Pātea, ngākau back in Taranaki once again.

Past Whareroa, and the Waimate Plains
onto Riemenschneider Strasse 8, my 'retired' parents.
(The council never did change it officially either).
One cosmopolitan day we will awaken multilingual

Pāteanui a Turi
For My Wairua

Laying your burdens down as you reach Mana Bay.

Mana as.

The expression of Tangaroa is confronting, authoritative and majestic.

Mana whenua can smell manuhiri from a mile away, with their ignorance and innocence, trying to catch a wave-

but only catching thrashings.

Where did you and the haumi pull up, ol' Turi?

Did you rest along the river mouth, the calm before the storm? Did the burden begin with the journey and end with the destination?

We can feel the rest you felt today.

Did you walk towards the township dreaming dreams of prosperity and abundance?

I remember driving around the bend and seeing, feeling, breathing... home. Kupu escaped me, tears welled up in my eyes.

I felt release from the great burden, leaving one life for the next. Unsure where the calling would take us, but certain it would only get better from here.

Maybe better is the wrong word. It has certainly had it's challenges along the way, as we try to find our way. Is this how you felt, Turi?

Did you ever feel lost Turi? Did you ever feel such contentment and yet much discomfort at the same time?

If you stop and take it in, you might experience the rest this land has to offer. Locals talk about the death of this place, but there is a lot of life left in these old bones.

Inner Child

For My Wairua

Have peace, inner child.
I hold you close
in the places where our Tupuna exist--

You are safe.

Have peace, inner child.
I embrace you in my arms as you search for a home-
You have a home with me.

Have peace, inner child.
There are stories to be shared and stories to be heard--
You have my undivided attention.

Have peace, inner child.
Our past and present spans a lifetime--
You hold the key to our Whakapapa.

Insufficient Funds

For My Wairua

You found me at overdraft--
exceeding my limits for you.
Always believing that the next week would be different,
that you'd return what you took,
but we keep going in to negative.

It was unarranged, insufficient,
never expecting to live from week to week.
The cost is becoming unbearable, it all adds up---
this life of mine.

Charging unauthorised fees, we can never seem to find.
Something always comes up, and we always 'make it work'--
I make it work by drinking
bottles of wine without thinking.

If you'd let me, I want to show you how great I am.
I'll suck it up for you, put it on my credit card for you.
I might even Instant Finance that for you,
show you how much you mean to me.

Let me get that on my tab for you.

Taiohi Aroha
Name Withheld

Me pāhea taku aro ki te karaehe?
He mita noa te tawhiti atu
Ko ō ngutu ka pērā ki taku mahara
te whero whero i ō pāpāringa
he hunga aroha huna tāua
nā tēnei mātauranga ka oma tōku ngākau
Kei te pupuhi ahau

Moe mai rā
i a au e kōrero ana
Kei te whakatikatika noa ahau i ngā ārai
i runga i ōu ū tahanga.
Kare te aroha e titiro tata...
Ka taea e au te titiro ki tō tinana mō ngā haora maha
ō pihinga reka
tōu raorao huna
te ana tapu

Te ohorere o te ataahua i homai e koe ki ahau
te hiahia e rere ana i roto i ō tatua toto
ko tēnei tāku e hiahia ana
Ki te tukituki i ō takutai kia ngaro atu tāua
Te harikoa me te mataora o ngā atua
Mō tētehi ahiahi, ko tā tatāua taonga

E ai ki a rātou he tamariki tonu tāua
Ko enei kare
ehara i te mea pono, i te tika rānei
Erangi tenei aroha
e ora tonu ai tāua
Ka haere ahau ki te kura
kia kite i a koe e tōku hoa aroha
tōku ūkaipō, tōku whakaora.[27]

---

[27] TEENAGE LOVE. How can I concentrate in class?/You are metres away/ Lips as plump as I remember/ the red blush in your cheeks/ we are secret lovers / this knowledge makes my heart race/I am throbbing. [v] Sleep on
while I am talking/ I am just arranging the curtains/ over your naked breasts/ Love doesn't look too closely...
I could gaze upon for hours / your delectable curves/ your hidden valley/ the sacred cave. [v] the urgency of beauty you gave to me / desire which flows in our blood/this is what I want/ To pound your shores until we are lost /The bliss and rapture of the gods/ For one afternoon, it is our prize. [v] They say we are still children/ these feelings are not real or right / but this love keeps us alive / I go to school to see you, my lover/ my source of sustenance, my salvation. (English translation by Trevor M. Landers).

Te Tangitangi o Kiri
Kiri

Ko te wahine e noho kore aroha ana karekau he oranga.

He anga totoro ki runga i te poroi pākarukaru o te roimata,

te mamae me te mamae...

Ko te ngāwari anahe ka huri te kuini makariri

ki te tino kotiro kua pakaruhia ngā ārai, kua huri ngā maunga!

Ko te ngāwari tētahi o ngā tūranga e hanga ana i te wahine i

roto i te wahine...

I whakaarahia i runga i te ngāwari, he rerekē anō tana kanapa.

Ka rite ki ngā ringaringa, nga waewae, ngā ūpoko...

He mea motuhake te kanapa.

Nō runga i te mea kua pono, kua kī te koakoa.

Kaore he poke me ngā momo whakakapi.

Kaore he moni me ngā painga ka taea te whakakapi i te ngāwari

Te ngāwari kua raranga mai i te aroha pono.

Ka tere te memeha o te wahine i te wā e tino kore ana te aroha.

Ka ora ngā tokorua mō tētehi ki tētehi

ehara mō rātou anō.

Ko te wahine e tika ana kia koa.

E whakaae ana koe?

Ko ahau tēnei wahine.

Ko ētahi kihi anō.[28]

---

[28] KIRI'S LAMENT: A woman who lives without tenderness is lifeless/A shell
stretched over a fragile ball of tears, pain and suffering/ Only tenderness turns
the cold queen into the very girl for whom barriers are broken and mountains
are turned![v] Tenderness is one of the foundations that form a Woman in a
woman/ Raised on tenderness, she even glows differentl/ Like the same arms,
legs, head/ And the glow is special/ Because it is filled with real happiness. [v]
Without impurities and various surrogates/ No money and benefits can replace
the soft tenderness woven from sincere love/ A woman is rapidly fading away
when she acutely feels a lack of affection/Couples live for each other, not for
themselves/ A woman deserves happiness/ Do you agree?/ Some more kisses
(for you) [English translation by Trevor M. Landers].

Ko Norm Broughton te kaiwhutupaoro pōkākā

Trevor M. Landers

Adrian, e mōhio ana mātou Ka taea e ia te purei whutupaoro,

Mō Taranaki, Wellington me North Harbour hoki

He ruānuku ki Hicks Park, ki Onewa Domain rānei

Te tianara iti. he pukenga hīrakaraka, te waewae kanikani.

He ika rerekē a Norm te Pōkākā; ka rite te rahi o ngā hūhā ki

te merengi; Ki ngā popoiangore e rua rānei!

Ka tākaro ki te tuarua-rima waru mō te kura tuarua o Pātea

He kaioma mārōrō me te kairutu wanawana hoki.[29]

---

[29] STORMIN" NORM BROUGHTON: Stormin' Norm Broughton. Adrian, we know can play rugby/ for Taranaki, Wellington and North Harbour also/ A mercurial wizard on Hicks Park or Onewa Domain. The little general, silky sskills and dancing feet/ Stormin' Norm was a different kettle of fish/ Thighs the size of watermelon/ (or) like two leopard seals!/Playing at second-five eights for Pātea High School/ A muscular runner and a frightening tackler too. [Whakapākehatia: Trevor M. Landers].

E kai, bro!

Name Withheld on request

In homage to Brian Potiki's poem, 'Tony'

E kai, bro!
it is me rapping the door
I have kina, mussels
& some smoked kahawai
a dozen Taranaki bitter cans,
no crate these days---stick it in the fridge
Ae, only a couple for us today.

I see your Tino Rangatiratanga flag
Fluttering next to the pennon of the 1835
Independent United Tribes out front
and is that a Ngāti Ruanui banner too, bro?
  Tēnā koe e hoa
  Tēnā koa kia kite anō tōku hoa
You greet me at the door
Mop of frizzy hair spilling out of your trademaek fedora
Your body dripping in tā moko ink
Like the face of the past & future
You are contemplating your mataora
Your teeth gleam, eyes glittering
Good to see you brother!

I enter your whare. Is this *Nekenekehia Tukua?*
a Wharehoka Smith installation; pondering: if Māori designs
permeated across Aotearoa. How cool would we all be?
Go hard artists, interior designs
Drop that icongraphy into our lives
Bring it on! Have another kuku!
We are sitting, but plates disappear
  Your missus is efficient, cuz.

We were scoffing Kaimoana looking for a bottle opener
The lemonade cap has cross-threaded itself
It is a shandy afternoon in the ripe plum of summer
A time for savouring; old friends, old favourites
Rekindling all the laughter and tears
  It feels good to be in your orbit, bro
A gravity we both feel.

At the Marae
The tūpāpaku lies serene
Your kuia was a sweet old lady, no doubt.
I keep seeing the art of Shane Cotton and Seraphine Pick
Memories returning like urūruroroa (dragonflies) near the
river
Sparked by the tangihanga and the dreams we shared
  She is going to eternal rest bro, she deserves that.
We'll hongi and haruru the manuhiri
But at your table, we both feel the resonance and unworldliness
of true friends.

Breeder Boy II: Manu Bay Redux
Phil Kawana

Pony-tailed Breeder Boy

with leather jacket

& caffeine-studded eyes,

buzzing off Cafe Girls,

with their funky clothes

and done-that shoes.

He's window-shopping

to pass the day,

his life lent shape

by glimpses of dreams,

by a face with Hope,

by a meeting with angels.

Breeder Boy unties his hair

and becomes Tribal Herbsman.

There are pinprick burns on his shirt.

And the sun is shining

somewhere beyond this Misty Morning

that is half-Marley, half-Monet, and is passing

slowly into afternoon, easing

into the day like his hands

along the thighs of a beautiful woman

late one night in Manu Bay.

The soft clouds taste the sky

with candyfloss tongues,

and Breeder Boy smiles knowingly,

slips his fingers into the earth,

and lifts his face to the sun.[30]

---

[30] The original version of this poem was published in a 2003 anthology called Whetu Moana, which features some of New Zealand's finest Māori and Pasifika poets. With the permission of the author we suggested some very minor changes to the original poem. We suggested swapping Lyall Bay out for Manu Bay and reflecting the change in the title for inclusion in Ngā Pūrere Kapohau . After tracking Phil down, we are delighted to include this special version of the original poem.

He Whakataukī: A prose-poem response from the carpark of St. Joseph's School, Pātea to the great people of Pātea

Trevor M Landers

He kokonga whare e kitea, he kokonga ngākau e kore e kitea. A corner
of a house may be seen and examined, not so the corners of the heart
Kare e taea e tātou te kite i ngā whakaaro me ngā kare-a-roto
o ngā tāngata, nō reira, me atawhai me te ngākau aroha. We
cannot see the inner thoughts and emotions of a person, so we
need to be kind and compassionate.
He riri anō tā te tawa uho, he riri anō tā te tawa parā
The functions of the heartwood are one thing: hose of the sapwood
(pulp) another
Ko te tangata e rangatira ana ki ōna kare-a-roto, ka pai ake ki
te whakahaere i ngā raruraru. A person who has mastery over
their emotions better able to deal with conflict.
Ahakoa he iti kete, he iti nā te aroha
Although the basket is small, it is given with affectionate regard
Pērā i te pounamu utu nui, he rite tonu te hiranga o ngā mahi
iti ki te koha utu nui. Ka āwhina te tauutuutu ki te poipoia te
mōhiotanga me te hāpor. Like precious pounamu, small acts
of kindness are just as important as expensive gift. Reciprocity
helps to build understanding and community.
He hono tangata e kore e motu; kāpā he taura waka e motu.

Connections between people cannot be severed whereas those of a canoe-rope can

He mea nui te manaaki i te whanaungatanga kaha mō te oranga o te whānau katoa. Me whakanui tātou i ēnei hononga, i ngā wā pai, ā, i ngā wā kino hoki. Ka āwhina tēnēi ki te whakapakari i ō tātou hāpori mō te whanaketanga i ō tātou oranga. Cherishing strong relationships is vital for the wellbeing of all whānau. We must value these relationships, in good times and bad. This helps us to strengthen our communities and further improve our collective wellbeing.

Taku hei piripiri, taku hei mokimoki, taku hei tāwhiri, taku kati taramea. My necklace of scented moss; my necklace of fragrant fern; my necklace of odorous shrubs; my sweet-smelling locket of Taramea

Ko te Taramea tētehi tipu matapopore me tōna he tarawai kakara reka, he. hinu māpuna hoki. Nō reira, me aroha noa tātou kiki a tātou i ngā wā katoa. Taramea is a highly prized plant with a rich aromatic sap and perfumed oil that was highly prized. Therefore, we must cherish people always. [31]

[31] These whakatauki are excerpted for artistic purposes from Leonie Pihama, Hinemoana Greensill, Hori Manuirirangi and Naomi Simmonds, He Kare-a-roto: A selectionof Whakataukii related to Māori Emotions, University of Waikato, Hamilton, (2019), pp.1-16. They are indented and italicised. These are accessible at: https://www.waikato.ac.nz/__data/assets/pdf_file/0008/480788/He-Kare-aa-roto-Full-Booklet-for-download.pdf

Ngā Rohe Tuarua

Te Ingomuna

Ko te kapua puru ki runga i te mounga (Lenticular cloud over the mounga) ©
Mātātuhi Taranaki, 2022.

E rua ngā iwi rongonui

Ngaa Rauru Kiitahi ki te tonga

Ngati Ruanui ki te raki

ngā kaihoko matua o te hitori

ina koa i ngā pakanga o whenua

te muru raupatu mai i Parininihi ki Waitōtara

ka titiro whakamua mātou ki o mātou whanaunga

te whakatipuranga

te puāwaitanga

te arangatanga ahurea nui

ake ake ake!

Ko te wā tēnei mō tō uri

ki te kanapa me te arahi i te huarahi mō te katoa.

TE KAAHUI O RAURU

Whakaahurangi
Michele Leggott

we were coming round the mountain
dog in the footwell   playlist old favourites
we were driving six white horses
through Tataraimaka Ōkato Warea Rāhotu
Carmelita Spanish Stroll Tipitina
through Pungarehu Ōpunakē Pihama
Dallas Talk to Me of Mendocino Who Do You Love
a summer morning to ourselves coming round the mountain
which has its cloud cap on and changes shape   with each twist
of the dial A Case of You Black Coffee   Prince and KD Lang
Hickory Wind and Our Town   Gram Parsons and Iris DeMent
we turn inland across the plain to Eltham Mountain still on
our left the cheese factory isn't open   it's Saturday
Erma Franklin Piece of My Heart   Aaron Neville Tell It Like It
Is we turn north for Ngaere and come to Stratford
Grace Jones La Vie en Rose   Bettye Swann Then You Can
Tell Me Goodbye follow Pembroke Rd to the Mountain House
and the Plateau Etta James At Last   Amy Winehouse Love is
a Losing Game

she came from New Plymouth to Stratford on the early train
set out on horseback in a party of nine up the mountain track
for Lady Shoe Camp on the edge of the Plateau   close to Te
Popo Gorge   she collected wildflowers   sketched and painted
not at all five days and then the horses came to take them back
through the burning season   trees on fire understorey cleared
for pasture   smoke choking horses and riders   she wept
in the saddle and took her flowers into the sitting room of
Emma Curtis   who with her companions Sarah Arden Mary
Bayley and Eva Dixon   had climbed to the crater from the
eastern slopes the year before   returning to camp with Mary's
ruined shoe that one of the menfolk nailed to a tree did my
great grandmother Elizabeth climb the stairs to Mrs Curtis's
sitting room to admire the paintings the artist made from her
mountain flowers during the week she stayed on in the town
primula buttercup pearly everlastings pale blue harebells
small white celmisias not enough coins in Elizabeth's slender
purse to buy a picture but she drank in the delicate membranes
rendered in watercolour   remembering the flowers of her
own Welsh valleys

Fire and sword   chaos and ruin the child drowned   dead of
malnutrition or dehydration the forest recklessly destroyed
there has been such grief in this place I am in your hands
a wide-brimmed hat floats down on the books   the rohe   the
child's dark head such grief   so many shadows

Here you are   she says   I have been waiting all this time
I am in your hands a small flower in the crevice of a rock   face
turned to the sky desire path in the dark faintly luminous
I am in your hands

Ruaputahanga was a high-ranking woman of Pātea
travelling with her followers to the east of the mountain
on her way north to marry a Kawhia man   sometime later
leaving a husband and son   Ruaputahanga journeyed back to
her people the party camped one night on the slopes of the
mountain
Ruaputahanga lay looking up at the summer constellations
falling asleep with her face to the sky her followers withdrew
not wishing to disturb her rest   the campsite was known
thereafter as Whakaahurangi   and the old trail became the
Whakaahurangi Track

the word slips away and is replaced   innocently thoughtlessly
carelessly see you later alligator   in a while crocodile
for you I was aflame   a flame   What's the story morning
glory   never mind roller blind   a hat floats down on the
books   the map   the child's dark head where is that rohe
memories futile arms oh what a mess we made   what's the
word hummingbird   all for love mourning dove

they drive to the maternity ward in Miranda St

he waits for hours until their daughter is delivered   near dawn
on a spring morning in Stratford
fourteen months later he guns the truck south to Levin
dropping off the child with a beloved aunt   turns north again
to be at the hospital in Stratford before the second baby comes
the third trip in the truck I remember   dropped with our
grandmother in Brecon Rd my brother and I hear about the
new sister next day   from a phone in the Waitara maternity
home
it is a frosty morning in Stratford   a kerosene heater roars
themountainstandsoutsharpandclear waitingforitstravellers[32]

*

(*A drive around the mountain on a summer morning intersects with
an artist's visit to Stratford and the Plateau in 1890 and with an older
journey over the shoulder of the mountain by the woman from Pātea,
Ruaputahanga of Ngāti Ruanui, who rested one night with her follow-
ers close to where Stratford now lies. Birth and death come home to the
small mountain town with wide eastern horizons*).

---

[32] Reprinted with permission from Landfall, University of Otago Press (2022).

Te Whanga o Turi me ngā pūrehu kapohau

Trevor M Landers

Turi's Harbour, Pātea with wind turbines in the background, © Trevor Landers, (2021).

Before making landfall here

commander Turi, the kairungi of the Aotea

made a short rest stop in Ngāti Tū country

at Kaupokonui-a-Turi-i-te-Ariki-nui

where they camped overnight at Maraeturi

a place immanent in my bones.

At Te Whanga-a-Turi, Te Pou-a-Turi
high tide waves inundate
delapidated piles of maritime history
when Pātea was a major shipping entrepôt
touted even as a colonial capital
but for the treachery of the perilous bar

Juxtapositions then, wind turbines scything the air
green energy generation within a signature
the faintest imprint of coastal shipping
the ghostly apparitions of schooners
loaded to the gunwhales with colonial impudence.

Turi did not suit expansionist narratives
the cultural logic of superiority asserted
& the reclamation of mātauranga kore e kitea
these cultural understandings efflorescent
becoming visible, speaking the dialects of the ancients
to the 'moderns'; we can learn a lot standing here
ngā pūrehu kapohau, the turbine blades, spinning
heralding new worlds built on the foundations we keep.

Homage to Waverley

Source: © Trevor M. Landers (August 2022).

Iron throne, submerged

Michaela Nyman

This ship is of a curious kind, missing
its midriff
see how it chops the waves eats
chunks of seabed
sucks and dumps
like the waves at Back Beach and Fitzroy
past that shifty bar where Virginia got concussed
a wonder it even stays afloat

Who does the sand belong to anyway?
Trans-Tasman Resources had their eye
on extraction of vanadium-rich iron ore
off the coast of South Taranaki
50 million tonnes of sand per year
a bay hollowed out. The Supreme Court
said no, echoing locals and iwi

On average a tonne of sand equals 0.625 cubic metres
or 625 litres
on account of the iron's heaviness, it's probably a bit less
50 million tonnes is an 11-digit number of litres –
hard to even imagine

Vanadium is used for treating diabetes, high
cholesterol, low
bloodsugar, heart disease, tuberculosis, syphilis
takes care of tired blood
and water retention, can also be used to improve
athletic performance and prevent cancer

You'll find vanadium in space vehicles, nuclear reactors
aircraft carriers, pistons and axels, as girders
in construction
potters use it as pigment.

Wet-skinned we flap angels on the hot sand hold
        salty grains in our mouths let trace
elements seep into limbs, skin, blood, tongues

It's been aeons since we took a trip of any kind
sand trips all the time
calculating all the inner dimensions of a truck you end up
with a trip of sand or 450 cubic feet
so many feet in one single truck. [33]

---

[33] First published in the Spinoff, (May 2022).

going west II
Mike Oliver Johnson

Some come to this little place to sketch

a tree in the throes of the sky

I'm here for the upswing

of a pogo stick morning,

fresh as a cut lily

I pop in out of a dream

just to be here for a while

but all I can see is

the holy river of the Ganges

swollen with bodies

the air thick with the smell of corpses

and the blood of dead children in Gaza

flowing as soft as a lullaby into the sand

and I can't think straight anymore

can't hold thought upright

can't maintain a clear heart

I am smeared across the face

of too many years

with my fungal hopes

and running dreams

I resist everything that is blue

the lightness of my own step

resent my facile content

my eye, always seeking beauty

even in the dark torment of rock

I don't want to stick out

of the side of the world

like that bit of tree

hanging onto nothing

the skin of my life has cracked open

to pour forth grey river stones in abundance

and sorrows untold:

see how despair comes rolling home

like a drunk, muttering to itself

while joy takes off at dawn

and never looks back

ah, see, the tide always runs

with the wind backs up into our lives

I transcribe these notes

the morning after

a thrush outside my window never stopped singing.

The Strange Art of Letting Go (Waverley)

Trevor M. Landers

E Pēhipēhi ana angeau
Amongst a growing list of promises
I can't make my friends see me.
This weight will tether.
You can come back up again.
The faithfulness of gravity, of rebounding, the pendulous
loop, if only I'll stay.
E Pēhipēhi ana angeau

Kei te āwangawanga anō
When I walk down Weraroa Rd
it's almost as if it'll be the last
the trick of permanence seizes me
I start hoping again after this interregnum
Utes following all their stupid old lineages back
and forth---I don't know how to do it: hold their silly faces in
my hands. Tell me what awaits...
Kei te āwangawanga anō

Kei te raru te āhuarangi
I cried when I saw the photos of broken-hearted people. Later,
I had to cut the phrase out of my tongue: every poem wanted
to utter it...

If a record skips you bend low to greet it.
You greet it with a cloth and your own good breath.
Kei te raru te āhuarangi

Kei te muramura te rangi
The sounds of the wind turbines
ought to soothe us but the word 'scale' leaps out at us
like a hare expecting the gruff bark of a shotgun
still the milk tankers rip up these roads of indignity
Kei te muramura te rangi

kua arotakengia te kukū hāora
What's the Finnish word for pre-emptively missing something
so much you can't look at it.
Literal translation: green, green, green. You better learn,
earn that expression to rote
breath in fresh littoral air like a tourist might, the big bad
taniwha calls himself: emissions trading - some local farmers
shit themselves with panic and inertia. Denial: and old reo.
kua arotakengia te kukū hāora

Ko te rā tō tātou hoariri
I choose not to wade into a blanket of ignorance
out past the shoreline's certainty, iron sands lurking
Breathe in sleet, lie on the graves of reefs, bleach the lie. The
townsfolk pray for simpler ghosts and hauntings,
In lieu of a proper translation for my grief, I say: green, green,

green, until it cools enough to block out the harsher sun.
Ko te rā tō tātou hoariri

te maunu aituā
When disaster comes, some of us will stand on the rooftop
bellowing at the chimeric faces, ghosts.
Some of us will hold our heads.
Some will look for shards of water,
run our morose tongues along the floor.
The truth: under the topmost sand is another, darker layer,
damp with ocean's closeness.
People will beg to be buried in a cool grave.
A last reprieve from the unrelenting sun—sun—sun—sun-
bake.
te maunu aituā

Maranga! Whakaoho!
I say when, like the disaster hasn't started arriving,
like an over-eager guest to a barbecue, drinking unwisely.
There is trouble already brewing, even in sleepy Waverley, on
the road to Whenukura, and in Pātea beyond, without doubt.
Check the forecast.
Gulp the air greedily, let's remember how it used to be. Let's
teach our sacrificial children the art of letting go....I will miss
you like....
the live firmament of these lime trees.
Maranga! Whakaoho!

Autumn in Waverley

'The Awesomes': Thomas Perrett, Rangimarie Peeti, Ben Johnson, Tyler Holdsworthy and Leigha Johnston[34]

The leaves turn red, copper, orange.
    Old Jack Frost coats the ground
we delight, jumping into piles
    of yellowing leaves,
listening to their satisfying crunch
    the sound of new calves and lambs
        marooned into the world
           bleating for lost mothers
& in the late afternoon
    a shy sunrise peeks out
        at a fresh born day
      delivering us to school.

---

[34] Year 8 students at Waverley Primary School.

Misadventure on Omahina Road

Te Tuhi Holdsworthy

A turtled car on Omahina Road, © Te Tuhi Holdsworthy, 2021.

Like an overturned turtle

    abandoned car, ringed with Police tape

    misadventure written

    on a re-arranged bumper

attempt to defy the laws of physics

  spectacular failure to launch

    crumpled fenders

     a chassis coming back to kiss

      the driver goodnight

     before the rescue helicopter

   winched your battered body

to the asylum of an ICU bed at

Taranaki Base. You are lucky, sonny!

  Take heed, you were lucky, this time!

   Speed, reckless risk, nearly stole your

    grasp on the threads of this life

     severing the warp and weft

      of daily living, taken for granted

     as if an infinite resource

    that cannot be endlessly

   expended by whim

  gambled like a ticket at the Waverley Races.

Heedless of the shadow of demise,

upended in a split second

  misjudgement and recklessness

    so very nearly ending the story here on a   blood-stained
epitaph.

      Young man, slow down, you have time, your impotent
rage will temper, boy-racer slow down

      before you wrap yourself around

      an immoveable mound or

      plummet

      down a mossy ravine,

or head-butt a power pole at 130 kph.

Broken-down outside Waverley Motors

Katherine Joyce

It was winter
driving south
Eltham to Paraparaumu
between Pātea and Waverley
Heidi, the Volkswagen Passat GT
(plenty of miles on an over-wound clock)
she starts knocking and clunking
we limped into Waverley under duress
parked the stricken beast outside Waverley Motors
the best rain knows when to fall
it descends during the most banal of calamities
waiting for dependable Dad to come to the rescue
a long wait; a winter's night bearing claws
patina of frost latticing on the windscreen
a shrill and doleful wind whistling down Weraroa Rd
The AA service agent revives me before death
Perhaps a priest would have been better
all thurible and muttering the last rites softly.
But it is fixable, just not on this inclement light
not in the biting Waverley cold of winter.

The Old Waverley Railway Station

Sam Landers and Trevor Landers

Waverley Railway Station, © Trevor M. Landers, (October 2021).

The old station
marooned above the high tide lines
echoes with the distant clang of locomotion
daubed with unoriginal graffiti
waiting for the freight trains north to Fonterra
the clamour of excitable passengers
has faded like historical silhouettes
and chipped paint.

"Kia tere e whaea, we'll be late"

"Yeah, two drums of wire should about do it"

"The Blue Streak will depart this platform at 10.57am"

"Do remember the days when people used this line, Mum?

"We shall see son, Santa may buy you a trainset if you are good"

„Taihoa! Kaua e haea ēnei paara e tama! Ko te huruhuru tino pai o Romney i konei! Whakamahia tō kanohi me tō māhunga!, I tata tērā. Kororia katoa ki te atua i runga!"[35]

Ein deutscher Tourist zum anderen: „Hans, schade, dass es hier keinen Personenverkehr mehr gibt?" „Jah, Dieter! "[36]

"How you meant run a @#$%'g business if the train is late!"

"Deși este degradat, este foarte frumos, nu ?"[37]

"Honestly, Timmy, behave yourself or wait in the Buick!"

The voices, the footfall of patent leather shoes, work boots

The pleasantness of daily transactions, hub of activities

The cars and truck parked expectantly; only the payload differs.

The maudlin whirring tracks,

a chugging Diesel Loco approaches.

---

[35] AUTHORS' TRANSLATION: "Stop! Don't rip these bales lad. Finest Romney fleece here! Use your head and your eyes. That was close. Glory be to God above! "

[36] AUTHORS' TRANSLATION: Discussion between two German tourists:" Hans, isn't a pity there is no passenger service from here anymore? Yes!"

[37] AUTHORS' TRANSLATION: [A Romanian visitor]: Though it is dilapidated, it is very beautiful still, no?

The Old Railway Station: A Reprise
Sam Landers

Screaming and steaming it came to rest,
parades of people pondered the scene,
foreigners fleetingly flung off the machine,
it could only mean the Waewae Express.

Scents of fresh produce ran through the air,
dollars dished out on local goods and rides,
knick-knacks to be seen with every stride,
it could only imply the impending Waverley Fair.

Life carries on now without this transportation,
where once hordes of people, now rodents in their wake,
the wooden structure remains, and boy, does it shake,
it can only be the Old Waverley Railway Station.

Fonterra Tankers (Waverley)

David Sims[38]

Fonterra Tanker (Waverley), © Trevor M. Landers, (October 2021).

This might all end here
Because you see
I am a tanker driver trundling down the main street
of Pātea and Waverley in the small hours of the night
hundreds of litres of milk onboard
decelerating near a town near you,
engine-break disengaged as you quietly sleep.

Now, we are well-placed to make commentaries
on idiotic drivers attempting to overtake
a fully laden articulated truck near the brow of a hill,
or playing chicken in passing lanes
Of course, at such colossal weight we do tend to make a mess
of the roads & that we cannot deny.

---

[38] EDITORS' NOTE: David Sims is a pseudonym of a real Fonterra tanker driver whose real identity we have verified.

Arriving at Moeawatea

Trevor M Landers

Happiness is not   an endless gravel road
   stretching onwards towards infinity   through virgin natives
not always being so very much fun   if you don't mind a jostle   and
a jangle now   just when everything is fine   the pothole
strikes   because even in heaven,   they
don't ululate every day.
In the far reaches of the province   great stillness is upon us
if you don't much mind   a few dead possums
beseeching the road   or casual racism
in casual conversation   with innocent-looking upturned
faces
or such other unspoken improprieties   a little bush-blush bigotry
who can they detest   dandelioned-deadheaded hippies in
fern-frond hideaways   ramshackle rural housing   save
mast-head indignations   just keep driving, son,
Delta, and its various segregations   our foolish flesh is a heir
        even the arcadian idyll cannot escape.
        Stop and unwind
a quick lover's last kiss   makes the sad, solemn scene
inspirations, walking around   looking at everything
smelling wild flowers,   listening for the far off

burble of a river   the lure of having a

swim,

naked in a paddock bronze with hay,   middle of

summer

dry grass crushed underfoot,

the

tramp

starts

here.

Threads of Waverley

Naomi Fitzpatrick

I believed love was a long, bright thread,
stitching skin to tender skin, pushing through the calloused
places, binding us in untold ways. Love laced me into a
fabric—a soft garment or a quilt, comfortable, warm, easily
embraced—where I was integral, larger than my loneliness.
I once believed us so well-sewn we showed a seamless face,
a cloth woven whole but the underside was really exposed,
the seams not put under stress tests. With wear, ineluctably
comes tear, stains appeared, and durable material thinned
to gauze—then a rip, a rent, a hole, entangled shreds to the
point of frayed dissolution. You prefer spandex whereas I was
pure cotton. Love should not end dull and frayed beyond all
recognition and repair, nor should it begin with design, a knot,
a needle, and a trail of bloody puncture wounds. Sometimes
it ends liked ripped jeans or loosing buttons in the wrong
hands. Sometimes undressing is a cardinal sin, and at others a
carnal delight. What connects one person to another escapes
me now. I believed I was a long, bright unbreakable thread.
Smooth. Strong. Tough and resilient to make love last.
Just maybe.

I need new material.

Redefining Wairoaiti?

Panisa Pitigaisorn

1. (noun) Māori mame of a small town on the North Island of New Zealand. According to local legend, it is the birthplace of the Māori God of War, Uenuku, or is it Tūmatauenga? Today, it is known for producing the best goat cheese in the nation.

2. (adjective) related to either the God of War or the goat cheese produced in the northern part of New Zealand. Don't confuse them!

3. (noun) A long spear made of hardwood with engraved carving, traditionally used by Māori warriors between the 18th and 19th centuries.

4. (noun) The first day of the voyage, aka Embarkation Day.

5. (urban dictionary) A mumbled gibberish for "Where are our IT?" said by balding man who couldn't turn on his computer.

The Water at Long Beach, Waverley

P.J. Schaeffer

Yes, the waves will rise above us,
roll in great change
flooding through our houses
stripping beds,

sheets and pillows
drifting off like a plague of jellyfish.

It means to unhang
family pictures, lay
them down beside
the drowned,

carry off their bodies,
the pianos, the aquariums,
ordinary leaves like some palanquin.

Then the schoolchildren will swim
with mahimahi &
eels draping themselves around
silenced ceiling fans

and potted hoya nestle
in the limbs of taller trees
out of reach of traders and scalpers.

The large appliances
will float
through doorways
like ungainly sea mammals:
a dugong of dolphining whiteware
new collective nouns will be invented.

migrating, following
food, singing to each other
a song that says:
We bloody told you so!
adrift on flotsam
off the coast of Waverley.

The racehorse that became the Mayor of Waverley in 3.18.90 flat

Trevor M. Landers

A six year old chestnut gelding, sired by Blarney Kiss
        out of Malrayvis
the bloodlines an augury, Irish Lancer & Messmate in the mix.
Only winner of the Wellington
        & Melbourne Cups in the same fateful year, 1983.
           Famously bought for $1000 by Waverley
     sheep farmer, Snow Lupton,
           the horse was called simply 'Kiwi'.
Won the Wellington in a come
from behind close finish, covering the ground in 3.20.29.
At Flemington
       for the Melbourne Cup
         considered a rank outsider.
Jockey Jimmy Cassidy
       settled the nerves at the rear, 24 in the field,
     At the turn
     500 metres to go
         2nd last, in front of the hapless *Amarant*,
running lame.
At the judge, won by a length,

punters, commentators, astounded.

Then came that replays of that immortal line:

'and here comes Kiwi out of the blue' as he mowed down the

pretenders. Lupton admitted,

Kiwi *'rounded up the sheep'* as part of his conditioning,

the rank underdog became an overnight sensation,

jubilation in the Clarendon and anywhere a thirst is

capable of being slaked.

In 1984, controversy struck,

Kiwi scratched on veterinary advice,

Snowy adamant she could have

run,

another Australian

underarm tactic?

Lined up in 1985, finished a creditable fifth.

In 1986, almost a repeat of 1983's heroics

a blistering final run before

pulling up lame with the line in sight.

Later, the same year he represented New Zealand

at the Japan Cup, Tokyo

finishing a game fifth in rarefied company

afterwards, retiring, with 60 starts, 11 wins, 8 seconds,

pulling in nearly $550k, ah but the

memories! Kiwi slaying them

on the first Tuesday in November,

two nations agog,

Geez, that was gold, mate.

The Pride of Waverley, 'Kiwi' with Jimmy Cassidy aboard, winning the 1983 VRC Melbourne Cup in sensational fashion. © Melbourne Age, (November 1983).

'Kiwi'

Sonja Lawson

Way back in the 1860s many acres cleared

In the Waverley area the Luptons cheered

Farmland areas needed a lot of breaking in

Hard work paying off with money in the bin

In the early 1900s Ewen (Snow) & Anne Lupton met

Carrying on the farming tradition with their sweat shed

On his farm Snow used horses to do stock work

A quiet, gentle farmer, worked hard so muscles hurt

The Luptons, on training horses they were very keen

Looking for that wonder horse; the greatest to be seen

In 1979 attending Te Rapa Dalgety bloodstock sales

Snow and Anne looked around sitting on hay bales

Anne really wanted a Blarney Kiss bred colt

Had to be coloured chestnut with no fault

The Luptons did find the perfect horse

Who cost $1000 very cheap of course

Naming the strapping young colt; who had a say?

The Luptons would name the horse in the usual way

Making a short list of preferred racing names

Quality would run through the horse's veins

The name Kiwi suited the horse to a tee

A nice simple name for the chestnut TB

Kiwi 's racing career started at 3 years old

With his chestnut coat glistening like gold

Kiwi did show a lot of promise as a young horse

Winning his 2nd race at the Stratford racecourse

With only 2 more races and Kiwi was turned out

Snow let Kiwi grow on the farm without a doubt

As a four-year-old racehorse two more wins Kiwi had

Including a win over 2200 metres which was not bad

Turning Kiwi out again to relax and mature

Back as a 5-year-old Kiwi would win for sure

Starting three times for 3 wins Kiwi was back

Including the Waverley Cup on his home track

Both Snow & Anne did deliberate and concur

The Wellington Cup was the next target, for sure

Racing in the usual bridle with snaffle bit

The usual jockey being Jim Cassidy riding Kiwi again

Storming home from last to first others watched in vain

Not long after the home win Kiwi was spelled once again

Making sure Melbourne Cup entries showed Kiwi's name

Despite entering Australia's famous & prestigious race

The Luptons would keep Kiwi on farm as his usual base

Kiwi was flown over to Australia only days before

Not racing beforehand but punters wanted more

The Australians always liked to have a good look

But the Luptons did not follow the record book

Kiwi was kept rurally in country farm bliss

Kiwi's nature was solid---how could they miss?

Kiwi was sighted half an hour before post time

Everything went to plan, and Kiwi was fine

Jim Cassidy knew exactly how to ride the race

They raised to win, not just to place

As on the first round at the winning post

Kiwi was last but the jockey let him coast

Last at the 800 metres Jim and Kiwi; would glory be?

Kiwi winding up for the huge raucous crowd to see

A great burst of speed from around the outside

Kiwi giving the triumphant jockey an awesome ride

The race announcer hardly had time to see

Kiwi sweeping past the 2 leaders, effortlessly

After the awesome win, Kiwi was the star

His amazing run was among the greatest by far.

Like Sisyphus

Katherine Joyce

she who wrapped what little she had in a worn scarf, not from
Burbury, more like the red shed,
walked for two days and two nights
under the glare of the sun

    the gleaming skull of the moon

she who loved the country with its green spirals, timber
dwellings, its summer dust and grit
the spinning wheel where she sang of Sodom

    while twisting harakeke and fleece

the pasture of a forever-unnamed woman who prepared a kai
for two strangers
baked rye bread over a low fire
    roasted lamb dipped in salt (and not the pink
  Himalayan jazz either)

she who lingered and looked back
rough hands shading her eyes
she who lingered and turned

worn from hours of walking

Watching her neighbour Sisyphus push quicksilver up a hill
like a mercury farmer, only to watch it bead down
the hill again.

She did not mean to disobey, simply tired of men's banal
orders, tired of a harsh god's lack of answers,
the uncaring silences, the tyranny of her longings.

Sisyphus will keep climbing pointlessly
    until his Waverley farm is
    swallowed by the sea
  & Lot's wife dissolves back into the ocean.

The Museum of Magnificent Motherhood
'Julia'

The Museum of Magnificent Motherhood is free on Fridays. I go with Aislin, who is also not a mother,

though she carries around a bag of needles
she bought years ago from a woman from

Tuvalu, who everyone called Bubsy. Aislin gave names to each of their lean metallic bodies as if they are her children. They are.

We start in the avant-garde art area where Sorrow for Suffering is the theme. We are encouraged. Most are from errant children apologising for misdemeanours

with sad, over-wrought faces that piques a steely cold rust in my nulliparous heart.

Aislin tells me about her dream last night, where a birthmark became a stigmata, gushing dark red blood
and some strange feeling there was something wrong with her clitoris.

She asks me that I think it means.
Displacement I say, conscious of hurting her non-mothering

feelings.

We walk on.
The next salle: 'Lost moments'
the opportunity costs of motherhood
dreadfully insensitive in the present company.

Back towards home
the empty playground of Waverley School
mocks our twin predicaments.

Let's wait for the next sausage sizzle.

Meconium & Merineum (Outside Dallisons, Main Street, Waverley)

Trevor M Landers

Hygge incarnate

    to abolish all fevered oppressions

   to alleviate all deep-seated anxieties

  a universal liberation from fears

    real and imagined

   to slay the invisible insidious forces

      massing on your pillow before fitful sleep.

Trucks trundle along Weraroa Rd, SH3 convulses into tremor,

these Leviathans emitting seismic shocks

    Behemoths of Fonterra and the haulage firms

      heavy imprint on brittle, pot-holed roads

        the price of the white gold-rush

        & amnesia about high-speed rail

        for the scent of the shelves in Dallisons.[39]

---

39   Meconium is the first motion of a newborn.Merineum is a Norwegian portmanteau of merry amd perineum, and used to describe the week between Christmas and New Year. Hygge is the Danish concpet of cosiness and conviviality engendering contentment and well-being.

The garden at dusk

Tony Beyer

at this time of year, the warmth
has stood in the yard
all afternoon into evening

once the sun departs
the flower-heads hold still
attaining for the moment their true colours

a comfortable hour for watering
in loose clothes
in improvised footwear

European at least by ancestry
we prefer to control
these uninterrupted spaces

borders defined
by selective plantings
random interlopers eliminated

yet the whole world
belongs to everyone and we

may need now to begin to be open

Advice to a Medical Student

Te Tuhi Holdsworthy and Trevor M. Landers

Ahahaha! That made me chortle out loud.
It is a matter of mild ambivalence; I was just
clarifying.... your bravura is not in doubt
the membership of that sorority, n=1
I urge you to resign today.
My generalist advice is K I S S.
Disarmingly simple, and therefore
easier for the analytical brain
to mollify or militate
the implications may seem so clear or disappointingly
opaque, it is not more ornate, arcane or recondite
but most truths have some universalisms attached.
However, its apparent simplicity
should not dissuade you
from exploring these abyssal depths
arterially discovering its lambent truths,
liberating you from the gnawing doubts
the little mind-mice that plague and pester
harass and harry your waking hours.
Next time you climb the Lindo Fergusson steps
dwell for a time, you only have the present,
today---- do not overload it with fripperies and frivolities.

Fear is not your friend.

Friday Night Free for all

Name withheld by request

It starts after 7pm
a flotilla of utes
covered in dust and cowshit
the unshaven, the shaven
the after-shaved,
the bold eau naturelles
at least four men to every woman
around the pool table
it is a real sausage fest
the scent of desperation
offset by a few top shelf lubricants
& the tang of testosterone
and a few libations
which helps everyone
if you follow my gist.
Jesus, I still have to milk
in the morning.

Gauguin's Mandarin Garden on Fookes St

Alice Prendergast

Imagine if Paul Gaugin
washed up here
instead of Tahiti nui

                 would fertile land
         become the backdrop for scantily clad
                    women;

Ngā Rauru Kiitahi
might fulminate, lash out
when gallic charm proved   to be just another
tool of control. *C'est bon?*
           On thermal shifts, the Karearea rises
       like emissaries of an unseen army gulping air,
              all mistake and raw muscle.

After a crimson dawn
breathless blue of noon.
the pure turning of pages.
Art pretties up this blank wall.

           Take us, our shadows dragging behind,
             from one provisional idea to another
                without the flubber of thought,
                   just the mandarin scent

grasses shrink to a courtesy,

  archaic laws on the edges of prophecy,

seams of a spent pleasure.

            Or the ladder on its back sprouting tall weeds,

          parlours of old tasselled pillows and possum piss.

            What is the correct term for a poet's asylum?

Lá Côte d'azur

 may get better

media attention, press hype,

have better beaches the south of France.

              A better playground

          for the co-mingling of flesh and spirit

               but home is home

               & *La Poste* delivery from

                   Nice,

                 Toulon or

                 Cannes

          is perfectly reliable & there may be:

         colourful stamps for the philatelist.

Paroxysm at Long Beach, Waverley

Trevor M. Landers

I will look at intemperate sea
through the windows of hybridity
turbines in the distance
I foresee storms, tempests, and the return of the ravaging sun
If I can't sleep, I would be happy
for the tidal pull of your body of water.

I am on the headland
full daylight, a promise of a solar caress
just as useful a gleaming moon
when day transfers suzerainty to night, at last I'll sleep.

The sun and I are:
a complex relationship, old adversaries, spurned lovers,
one day the daylit sun might be too bright & violent, blistered
melanoma
I have already seen her at close quarters.

At its zenith, vertical in the sky,
the sun seers in minutes
remember the Coppertone sand-dwellers

running around without a care in the world
a splash of crème, little more than bronzing
each metronomic wave seemingly a sigh,
a fleeting word, a cry,
only a fugacious reprieve.

'Long Beach, Waverley'.   © Trevor M Landers, (December 2021).

Poetry tries to slow the traffic in Waverley

Anonymous

'Untitled' © Trevor M. Landers, (April 2022)

The trucks trundle through here

as if we won't exist

barely a lower gear engaged

& the bloody cars are no better

zooming along Weraroa Rd

as if it were blinking Silverstone

(though not a patch on Hamilton,

Le Clerc or Verstappen)

To the cops:

I would like to see

a blue cordon

some hefty tickets issued

and a bit of honest respect for our town

this is not a racetrack

slow down

you bloody mongrels

read the signs

and consider us,

the residents, for a change.

Waverley Moon

Trevor M. Landers

I shout with the rough calculus
　　of standing upright
　　　　let me move like a tide coming in
　engulfing you in brine-soaked embraces.

In the beginning, a moment
　　your mouth: soft petunia, rose murmur,
　　　sugared breath, a warm entrance:
　　　　　a toast to divine anatomies.

　Our bodies are their own voices
　　witnessing, given testimonies
　　　　to ancient euphorias
　　threading the hallelujah daisy chains.

Fly among twinkling clitoral stars
　　hear a forename intoned breathily
　　　let us reside under an ecstatic celestial moon
& ponder the enormity of this fleshy universe.

　Ask the tamariki
　　what the new moon requires of us
　　this skin bright world in glorious flame
　　　　　if you just hold still for the Waverley Moon.

The Big Sun

Trevor M Landers

-For KJH

With the artfulness of bookbindery
Your fingers interlock mine in *arpeggio*
Love praises dextrous digits as the *fraxinella* love ash.

Neither a haven for gourmands nor gossipmongers
A quick stop, a slow dalliance, lust's malassimilation.
The waitress horrent with a cuppa *majolica* & lemon slice

as her *paterfamilias* wanders in, a portrait of Rodd & Gunn
a dozen sapid cakes momentarily abandoned, subtle glances.
An order of *tournedos* breaks collective gaze, observances end.

Yes, my darling, my eyes can canoodle your countenance
even from three paces, the poet can be lethal given propinquity
Sometimes the logorrheic need not to utter one sublime word.

Hail the CWI

Janet Hunt

You would not expect it
here in the city
where a bearded academic
born & raised elsewhere
is giving a nod to
     the CWI

You would not know
unless you were there
how vital it was:
—it was everything for
     those women

Each alone on the 100-acre farms
   where soldier-boy husbands
     with no more idea
   of family life
   than a barracks or barroom
     were growing up
     with the century

You would not know
how weekly meetings
in cold hall or warm house
talking | showing | knitting | sewing
cancelled the
screaming baby
the shouting man
    the rain and wind

You would not know
how monthly meetings in
a garden
to swap cuttings and seedlings
& walk in the sunshine
kept the monster at bay
upheld
the civilised world

Ruru

Bill Direen

From deep within the snuffling
slow-whorling bush
pulsing with its own conspiracies
the long-distance wooing of ruru
beneath a paraselene moon

Mai i te hōhonutanga
o te ngahere pūhoi
e panapana ana me ōna ake whakapoapoa
ko te aruarunga o te ruru kei tawhiti rawa
i raro i te marama kātoretore.

Waxeye

Bill Direen

Dapper little assassin

poised on a swollen-jointed stem

among terrorist eyeholes of grub-eaten kawakawa

darts to its dolmade

too bad about that worm within

its ends a wave helplessly

tongued and swallowed in a wink of silver

He kōhuru āhua pai

ka taurite ki runga i te kakau hononga uruumu

ki te kawakawa pūareare, he pōtae pūāhuru, kaingia e te anuhe

ka rere tere ki tana hōtiti kaimanga

hei aha te anuhe o roto

ka poroporoakita ōna pito e rua

ka kowhakina, ka horomia,pērā ki te uira hiriwa

Farming outside Waverley

Michelle Young

There is no grass more lush

here the girls feast on prime clover

the very finest quality perennial rye grass

sloshed in the vat each milking

We love this life

and thus far, it loves us back

& the rural life

is second to none, let me tell you.

Glanton Navarian Blair with two farmers, Source: © Cliff Shearer

Dancing with The Shabby Old Lady of Waverley under the Spring Moon equinox
Jacqueline Högler

Dancing with the shabby old lady of Waverley

under the light of this planet; intoxicating fun

she stands dressed in tatty off-white gown

the light glinting in her windows; a twirl and a jig,

helpful for body and mind; the soul and heart sing

wherever you may find yourself ---a crepuscular sky, the

moon rising luminously shouldn't take surmising, wrangle

some friends, ignite a fire, snare a mandolin, *'ukulele* or lyre

singer, drummer; praise the spring! Soon the summer moons

shall shine, gaze into a stellar sky! Rejoice! Follow constellations

like dance steps; let your body go in gravitational orbits, still

the shabby old lady looks on impassively. Let your spirit flow,

your ego go, excitements of the dance; precious pleasures of

the flesh, embodied joys to be felt even if by creak of morning,

the shabby old lady is wood and architecture again.

The Shabby Old Lady of Waverley, © Trevor Landers, September 2022

Lost at the Waverley Racecourse

Trevor M. Landers

I must have been aged barely four
Colleen and Roger had the day off
from Manaia Convent School
so we went to the races, our parents deciding
the totalisator was a lesson in the mathematics of chance
and our absence wouldn't be arithmetically detrimental.
At Waverley, the old grandstand, demolished now
but we used to race up and down it
collecting jettisoned betting slips like strange currency
as if they were a strange new lottery
each race issuing
a slightly different coloured 'currency' for us to hoard
and there must have been
some elegant way to win but it has been lost
to time & the fallibility of human memory.
It wasn't always as happy as those carefree days.
At my first visit to the Waverley Racecourse
I lost Mum and Dad just before lunch
and I was a very upset little punter indeed,

crying inconsolably

in the Stipendiary Steward's room.

It was before my 4th birthday, and I knew my name

I had stopped to pick up some betting slips

---a critical task---

and when I turned around there was a forest of adults:

none of them resembled my parents.

I remember the announcement over the Tanoy

'a little boy answering to Trevor has lost his parents'

and these was a few agonising lip-quivering minutes

until my parents collected me

& then there were no more tears.

Later, to assuage the upset

I got an ice-cream to ease the anguish

& a can of Fanta to underline it.

I think Mun felt worse than me

& Dad wanted to collect a 'divvy'

from the previous race.

At least a decade later, I returned

Dennis and I backed roughies with reasonable form

"We" finished up, Mum and Dad a few dollars down

But the thrill of galloping flesh thundering down

A home straight sprint,

The crowd rising and yelling like at the Praetorium

The victors triumph,

the vanquished spill betting stubs onto the grass

A harmless little flutter

but warm, cosy, incalescent remembrances

from that otherworld of vaporous memory.[40]

---

[40] For younger readers, the author notes horse racing was once a very popular social event, the Waverley races being a very popular country meeting on the Central Districts circuit.

Seasonality

Mike Oliver Johnson

We measure our lives by the seasons, the rhythms of earth and sky. They turn into time, and we build our stories around them. That was a springtime of hope...that was a winter of discontent...that was an autumn of huddled dreams... that was a summer of dried-up skies...that was the year of the flower. There is no need to mythologise, the seasons do it for us. Our stories take their flavours from the world around us; context confers meaning.

Pungarehu <> Parihaka <> Pātea
OTS

Pick you up!
The depth of every lahar drives us
the slow, rolling lux of it
the green lilt of the tongue
the pukana eyes too, churr!
every hillock compounds matters
the cluttered disarray of rocks
they too lament the sacking of Parihaka
but that is not the whole story

Let that pernicious mindset
be scattered to the wind,
directionless portrayed and named it, Bryce
the colonial psychopath
a needless bloodbath
acting with integrity is really not so hard

recollect diversions flung, intercepted threads,
spun directions left, right,
breathe tama!

before you forget

Consider the complications
which daily intercessions
you will take up,
the politics,
the pressures,
the poisons
consider now
the battering wind
your reeling mind
in a quake of history

Watch out!
The madness on the road
Ah! For a moments peace
Arrive in Pātea, maidens hand caressing
curling toes, in sweetest most exquisite delight,
to curl in mindless ecstasy
as day retreats to night
We have arrived.
Yep, we are here.

The Pōhutukawa Tree at Waverley Primary

'The Leaders': Zach Brison, Lily Howe, Macey Wakeling,
Theo Deadman and Madisyn Hapi.[41]

The Pōhutukawa Tree stands tall,
must be over 100 years watching over the schoolyard,
nearly as old as the school
(it turns 150 this year).

Big limbs stretching out like an embrace
from a venerable uncle or auntie
it flowers to signal summer
the tree ensnares unsuspecting children
to be, inevitably
rescued by school leaders.

This grand specimen
collects Tūī and fantails
& lures moths to unusual lairs
but best of all
great camouflage for hiding from the Principal!

---

[41] Mainly Year 8 students at Waverley Primary School.

A golden time to reminisce about
T.I.

How grand a moment to look up
from the green grass through the Pōhutukawa tree

the four of us, baby-toothed and primary-schooled
back when the sky was a big broad sky-smile

Do you remember how the sunshine flickered through
and we poor, naïve souls had neither hats or sunscreen

At little lunch and big lunch, we played tennis-ball tag
trampling the smaller shrubs, creating little pathways

The simple games we played that entertained for hours
The schoolyard intrigues that lasted for a gnat's whisker

Remember your school pals and your fun and games
One day it will bring you more pleasure than it did then!

Storm clouds over the Waipipi Wind Farm

Trevor M Landers

Here, they are farming the wind
betting on turbines
& the reliability of the puffy stuff
to turn blades
generate fresh income
harness greener energies.

Let us hope
that the regard
for the environment
is much higher
than the overlords
of milk in Whareroa.

The bilious clouds
build in the approaching sky
rollicking on in deep blues
thickening gray,
blackening toward rain
The giant's scythes
revolving

deftly slicing the heavy air.

August wordstar II

Mike Oliver Johnson

the first stars to appear

come to rest in your mouth

as sharp stones, talking becomes difficult

singing a memory; light, the province of shadow

soon words begin to congeal, congeal

into hard, glittering points

seeking ascension

into the constellations of spring

by dawn they have melted

where was I, exactly?

Butter

Michaela Stoneman

Here we are again, creeping
on tiptoes in our own home
pretending not to be
here to each other

       We all need to tap into the feminine
       sincerely look at
       frills of oyster mushrooms
       bush drenched valleys
       the velvet antler

Here we are again, stewing
like overripe apples
crumbling facades
full of codling moth

       The nature nurture debate
       can work both ways
       the flavour of favour all depends
       on which side you stand
       which team you root for

We all need to tap into the masculine
sincerely look at

270

marbled wood slab

mountain peak

the waterfall falling

> Here we are again, reeling
>
> our shared nostalgia running deep
>
> underground waterways
>
> sneaking above and beneath
>
> history is a crock of shit

Oh,

to be softened

as easily

as butter.

A unique landscape out the back of Opaki, Source: © Trevor M. Landers

Out the back of Opaki

Trevor M. Landers

the best kind of travel
a tiki-tour with time or itinerary
we find a sheep farm
at the end of Kaharoa Rd
driving away
we stop for the landowner
ask about the Opaki Hall
showing up on our map on my iPhone XIII
he grins, then grimaces:

"It burnt down
about thirty years ago
it was full of hay at the time
some bloody arsonist set a match to it
went up like a Roman candle!
You'd be hard pressed to find anything now!"

We drive further on down Kaharoa Rd
past an awe-inspiring series of cones
in a sheltered valley
dodging sheep, who clearly have right of way
out the back of Opaki.

The Member's Enclosure at Dallison Park

Evan Wander

The Grandstand at Dallison Park, Source: Trevor M. Landers (2022)

Ah Jock, we have seen up humdingers here
some real nail-biting last-minute clinchers

You'll remember that one when young Lennox scored
full-time well and truly up on the scoreboard as well!

Those dank, dour winter days, rugged up, hat and scarf
when our forwards plodded in the mud almost incognito

Yes, Jock, we have watched some doozies here alright
whistle's gone for you mate, but I'll be here next season!

Goddridge's Pharmacy, Source: ©Trevor M. Landers (2022)

Godderidge's Pharmacy (Waverley)

Katherine Joyce and Trevor M. Landers

In a dollop of retro chic,

completely unself-conscious

the pharmacy on the

main drag of Waverley declares:

Jumbo pictures, prescriptions, presents

whatever that might mean.

It is one of those

small town chemists

a cornucopia of Pharmacopeia

the kind of pharmacy

that might nominate itself for a

Pharmacy Museum. If it should ever close

worried Waverleyans will remember when:

clutter was elevated to a para-medical art form

crammed shelves were a medicinal form of commerce,

prescriptions,

pills and potions

came with trusted advice

and the balm of a friendly face.

The Hussey St Kai Box (Waverley)

Aroha Broughton

The Hussey St Kai Box, Source: Trevor M. Landers (2022)

Ka pai koe, te tangata atawhai

me ō rātou hoa tata pea

mō te manaakitanga

te āhua o te hāpori

ka āwhina i te hunga iti, ka rawakore rānei

ehara i te hara. He aha te hara kei Aotearoa

ka nui a mātou rawa, engari ka iti noa te tohatoha.

Nō reira ka mihi atu āhau ki a koutou i Weraroa nei

Nāu i waiatatia tōku ngākau.

The Old Haunted Tree on Otaute Road
Richard Woodfield

Strange!
    A tree haunted by restless spirits that refuse to pass over.
      A tree that is well over 150 years old. In the right wind
        you can hear the ghostly respirations
of militiamen
      slain in the battles against Titokowaru.
Some say the
      ghoulish groaning is the grisly last gurgle
of a suicidal soldier.
        Others say the soldier was slain beneath the boughs
      his blood splattered onto the bark.

Dahlias on the Table

Kristan Horne and Trevor M. Landers

You placed a dahlia in my
hand. We looked at each
other in the haze.
I gave you a long poem written
with the heat of our breaths
last bloomings in a walnut grove.

It was the waves at Mōwhanau
the sea in Waipipi
It was in the days of our beach
walks and wordless embrace,
time smouldered
the ink of our song,
snug in the bend,
sang this melody for lovers.

You said:
"Time was stilled red was the colour
of afternoons pressed in our hands"
and you wrote poems to me

from that unwinding weekend
a tribute to love and to laughs,
and to syllables & slurpable Tom Yum Goong.

We are 50 now and read with
the whippet on my lap. She
knows the art of songs
sung in the wind,
with every sigh of her lovely
brindle coloured breast.

Tomorrow he will bring
me no nearer to the sublime
who sang, once, to me, in the car
like a rock star mouthing Morrisey lyrics
driving towards Severn St
for reasons I now understand.

Daffodils in Waverley

Kataraina Murray

My friend Te Rauhui hates daffodils,
I love them.

Their brightness dazzles,
A call of spring arising.

Beauty and impermanence
Brightening our days.

The Holy Grail: The Cemetery Circuit in Whanganui

Luke Martin

I am sitting here

sweating over writing a poem

dreaming of riding the Cemetery Circuit

a speed demon

swerving around chicanes

motorbike fumes in my nostrils

the awesome power beneath me

A world champion from Pātea

It starts here, right?

Avarnt, my BFF

Marnie James

He can be annoying, at times,

the way schoolboys often are.

He listens impassively

kind when the prevailing wind blows.

We met at the Pātea Public Library,

I was 10.

I don't remember it well.

But he is generous and loving, I guess,

Now he had a poem written about him.

Pā Harakeke

Dee Doherty

We are woven,
you and I and the sky,
above and below,
a breath, a death,
we, tangata whenua,
ache and cry,
as coasts erode and kākāpō die,
we are flax, the almighty thread,
the strands of Māui's rope,
that can no longer harness,
the sizzling sun,
wilfully slowed on its course.
We have no choice,
but watch it raze,
each blade of grass,
each kōwhai tree,
and helplessly wait,
zs the jawbone sinks,
to the plummetous depths,
of our tumultuous seas.
Stand as, our ancestral hook,

dregs up the whītau hungahunga
we are woven,
you and I and the sky,
now we are frayed,
and tinder bone-dry.
The fire is lit,
there is less shade,
as harakeke smoulders,
let's raise our game.

On Tertiary Education Commission Business at the Waverley Golf Club Lounge (2003)

Trevor M. Landers

for my former tertery Education Commission colleagues

Hardly, Camp David and with few

    creature comforts, the Waverley Golf Course

  chosen not for salubriousness

      but equidistance between New Plymouth

        and Palmerston North

      and presumably, low frills, low cost.

Robyn presiding, with

      her venerable Lieutenant, the inscrutable JV

  a leavening agent with Tony, as wise as an oracle

    a true heart of unalloyed gold

offsetting Mary's pranks, the cheeky humour of Paul and Matiu

    arriving early, detour to Waverley

coffee and muffins at The Big Sun

  awaiting the brethren from Manawatū

    another chance to play happy families.

next year on the terrace, National Advisor

    looking homeward: Taranaki

A break in the rain

Tony Beyer

it has felt its wet way with soft touches
all over the veranda roof
and exposed parts of outdoor furniture

the canvas seats of chairs
will have to be tilted and drained
and some shoes brought in to dry

just briefly there is silence
like the pause between sentences
in a sermon

one perhaps about the green wood and the dry
and the intuition
that no earthly state is permanent

already the blackbirds
are reclaiming the sodden lawn
where standing water ebbs among the grass

their voices clipped
into a series of short clucks

evincing neither forethought nor recall.

The Other Waverley

John Kearns

Typical!
Northerners stealing our limelight
rejoicing in a horse imaginatively called 'Kiwi'
See a cortege of muddy utes doing ballet
Swandris on Weraroa Road
Sawmill workers clutching Andersons' pies
A parked-up sheep transporter
with a huntaway peeking imploringly out
No! Turn your attention away!

Nestled up off the Portobello Road
snuggly enjambed between Vauxhall and Challis
we were named for an eponymous Walter Scott Novel
are the boisterous home of Grants Braes AFC
2,426 of us in all, more women than men, you jokers
Perched right next door: notorious Victorian pleasure gardens
If you get my drift, and will follow me a little further...
nineteenth century libertines, lasciviously flaunting
a postcard from the Edinburgh of the south
we are the other Waverley
Waverley of the South.

What if Morrissey grew up in Waverley?

Trevor M. Landers

Morrissey, misquoting Oscar Wilde said, "Talent borrows, Genius steals" so we use this acknowledging Morrisseycentral.com © 2022

Morrissey would still have incongruously driven a vintage Farmall with a woven straw hat but may not be conjuring the subversive, broody élan of James Dean, or the swagger of a mythical Wisconsin dairyman.

He might have stalled in the dank dungeons of his angsty teenage bedroom, 'writing frightening verse to buck-toothed girls in Luxembourg,' confusing the postmaster-general no end, but ask him, ask him, because....

The 'Rusholme Ruffians' would have had to lurk by the old Waverley High School gates, negotiating the wind tunnels, which look nothing like a whorling Werlitzer

At 'the cemetery gates', Keats and Yeats might have been on your side, but Morrissey and Wilde might have been joined by Tuwhare, Bornholdt, French, Pirie, Marsh, Harvey and Baxter.

The *Screaming Mee Mees* and *The Mockers* might have played in the Waverley Town Hall but Cilla Black, Sandy Shaw and the New York Dolls would have not graced Weraroa Rd.

'The Queen is Dead' would still have been written with a sponge and rusty hammer, though readily available, would have been difficult to conceal from Customs and Immigration inspections on the way to Buckingham Palace.

'Suffer the Little Children' would not have been written; we have no Hindley and Brady and Saddleworth Moor; just a terrible history of child abuse and infant mortality that OT cannot staunch, and we blithely pretend that mostly that is an apparition or a spectre happening out of our purview, somewhere else where.

'Handsome Devil', 'Hand in Glove' and 'Reel around the Fountain' might have shocked the respectable farmer's wives who blanche at bdsm and the assault on the unassailability of heteronormativity. But in liberal progressive circles the songs would be passed around like dangerous contraband, or a *samidzat* by a clique of aficionados.

'The Headmaster Ritual' will resonate for those who attended school at a time when disciplinarianism was the leading pedagogical tactic and where small 'gangs' enacted very asinine peer pressure bullying tactics in and out of school.

'That Joke isn't Funny Anymore' could discussed more candidly now addressing as it does, depression and suicide like a milk tanker thundering through town at night.

'Bigmouth Strikes Again', 'There Is a Light That Never Goes Out' and 'The Boy with the Thorn in His Side' could all get a run on the jukebox in the Clarendon, or the pub across the road for impromptu karaoke.

The vegan and animal rights anthem 'Meat is Murder' would scarcely find favour around Waitōtara and would be an acquired taste in the surrounding area. Fabulous lyrics, and a jangly melody to prick our conscience about the treatment of other sentient, sensate beings, perhaps?

'Strangeways Here We Come?' Pāremoremo or Kaitoke for mockingly blasphemous lyrics, or if you take the parodying call to arms 'Shoplifters of the World Unite' too literally.

'The Vicar in a Tutu', he is not an eccentric, he just lives a garish life sliding down the banister, put your spare shekels in the cannister, as 'natural as rain' he jigs, jives, and jitterbugs out of the sacristy. A possibility!

'The Last night on Maudlin St', stammering without inebriation: 'truly.....I do love you', the street lights flickering, a final saunter down Brassey, onto Swinburne, expecting to see Lord Byron. Well no inconceivable.

Tētehi wahine o Ngaa Raaru

He wahine o Ngaa Raaru

Ko te wahine e noho kore aroha ana, karekau he oranga
He anga totoro ki runga i te āmionga pākarukaru o te roimata,
te mamae me te pōuri...
Mā te aroha raupī te kuini anuanu tini ai ki te kotiro kua
pakaruhia e ngā parepare, kua tūohu e ngā maunga!
Ko te raupītanga tētehi o ngā āhuatanga e hāngai ana e te
wahine kia wahine ai ia
Ki te poipoia i te raupītanga, ka rerekē mai tōna muramura
Ka rite ngā ringaringa, ngā waewae, te ūpoko...
Erangi he mīharo ake tōna muramura
Nā runga i te whakapono o tōna hākoakoa
Korekau ngā poke me ngā whakakapi
Tē taea te pūtea me ngā painga te tū atu i te raupītanga kua
rarangahia i te aroha pono
Ka tere memeha te wahine nei kore tōna rongo i te aroha raupī
Ka ora ai te taurua mā rāua tahi, ehara mā te kotahi noa
He tika kia hākoakoa te wahine
E whakaae ana koe? [42]

---

[42] ONE WOMAN OF NGA RAARU: A woman who lives without tenderness is lifeless/ A shell stretched over a fragile ball of tears, pain and suffering/Only tenderness turns the cold queen into the very girl for whom barriers are broken and mountains are turned!/Tenderness is one of the foundations that form a Woman in a woman/ Raised on tenderness, she even glows differently/Like the same arms, legs, head.../And the glow is special/Because it is filled with real happiness/Without impurities and various surrogates/ No money and benefits can replace the soft tenderness woven from sincere love/A woman is rapidly fading away when she acutely feels a lack of affection/ Couples live for each

Mahimahi i te poupoutanga o te rā

He wahine o Ngaa Raaru

Ka toremi taku hoa ki taku koharatanga,

me taku aroha.

ki te hiahia koe ki te wahine tūturu pēnei ki ahau,

ko te kawatau kia ruku ai

ki te ao pārekareka me te harakoa.

Ka mōrearea ahau ki tō hauora

erangi ka mate koe manahau koe.

KKa whakakīa e te wahine me te tane i a rāua anō me he momo

rauemi, he ngākau whiwhita, he hihiko ora. He tauhohe matū

he tauhohe tinana,

he ngangau whakatenatena kia hinga ai ngā rerekētanga,

kia pūmau te aroha ahakoa ngā ngoikoretanga

ko te aroha o te change to whakawhānautanga, ko ngā taiaki

taihemahema

ka onioni i te poupoutanga o te rā.[43]

---

other, not for themselves/A woman deserves happiness/Do you agree?

[43] SEX AT NOON: Sex at noon/my man will drown in my care, love and passion/If you need a real woman like me/then expect to plunge into the world of pleasant emotions and pleasure/I can be hazardous to your health
but you will die in bliss./A woman and a man fill each other with a resource, a passionate energy, a life motivation/ A chemical and physical reaction/ a surge of inspiration to overcome differences, to love even imperfections/the love of procreation/these are sex hormones/congress at noon.

Waiata o te Patupairarehe mō te rangatahi

Trevor M Landers

Maranga, e te hunga e moe ana

Whakapaia tātou, whakamatauria tō tātou tānetanga

Hurihia ki te hauauru, ki te tonga, ki te raki hoki

Nekehia te rangi me te whenua huri noa i Te Pou o Turi

Ka oho ake,

Ka wewete, ka wiri

Kia rongo te kiri i te tio o te hukarere hou

Kia tere ai tō waka mā ngā ngaru puahiri

Wi wi wi

Wa wa wa

Aro atu ō kanohi ki te rangi

Kapohia te kura huna

Whakahōnoretia tō māramatanga

Ki a Meremere-tū-ahiahi

Hei whakatīahotia i te ara ki te moana o Tangaroa,

Koia te atua ka kumea te tini maha ki tōna tauawhi, ki te pōuriuri mutunga kore

kua oho ngā manu. Kua tae te ata.

Rangatahi, koinei tō haora!

Tū māia, piki mai, kake mai!

Chant of the Patupairarehe for the Youth

Trevor M Landers

Arise you who slumber

prepare ourselves, prove our manhood

heave to the west heave to the south and to the north

move heaven and earth around Te Pou o Turi.

It awakens,

it loosens, shudders

haul toward the majestic mountain

that the skin may feel the tang of fresh snows

may turbulent thundering waves speed your waka.

Wi wi wi

Wa wa wa

cast your eyes heavenward

grasp the important knowledge

deepen your understanding

toward Venus, the evening star,

to light the path to the ocean of Tangaroa,

the god who lures many into his embrace, into eternal darkness

the birds have awakened. Dawn has come.

Rangatahi, now is your hour!

Stand tall, be confident, rise high!

Second Thought

Richard Reeve

The dark unloads on river, rock and plain,
and on the roof, we hear the rising rush
of wind, that drives the currents of the rain.

You, who would not give in, beneath the strain
of sixty years, now note the heavy hush
the dark unloads on river, rock and plain

(and still, amid the gurgling of the drain,
conceive a plan, a pattern to this flash
of wind, that drives the currents of the rain).

The meat case creaks, the sky's visceral stain
breaks open on the deer-degraded bush:
the dark unloads on river, rock and plain,

unloads its grudge. Pressed to a windowpane,
what slack impotence do your fingers crush?
But wind, that drives the currents of the rain,

but this, the beating deluge of the brain
against what lies beyond its bone and mush:
dark, unloading on river, rock and plain,
the wind, that drives the currents of the rain.

From Mokoia, Manutahi right through to Waverley

Name Withheld

and when you said

laughter is like a foreign language

i imagined that i was

teaching you how to

speak it

and when you said

making love was like divine spell

I felt the full force of a formidable fellatrix

teaching me how to drive under pressure

surfing left of the centre line, blissfully.

Describing Daffodils

Gary Bovett

in ruffs

a choir of

sweet sopranos

in the breeze

a school of glistening

minnows

in the rain

capturer of moisture

drops

ever the

harbinger of warmer

weather

ever the bringer

of hope

Waverley Skies

Jacqueline Högler

The clouds are having a party
I can see them
acting all nonchalant
throwing that red sky all over the place
the giants stand alone
with all the throngs.

Tooing and flowing
some dark sinister character
draws up closer, cumulus rising
the red bleeding into martyred violet
someone in a nondescript house on Suther St
keeps trying to draw the curtains

The clouds seems to emit a willingness
bestowing limitless possibilities
there are forces larger than the stupidity of man.
The rumble is a roar
These engines don't stop.

Assuring and seismic we huddle
---is all one can do in a cirrus moment
Gang on, amidst the nimbus turbulence
Just see if you land safely.
See if all goes well,
a thousand auguries.

It came to me in the Waverley Four Square (On Speaking Terms)

Jacqueline Högler

Cooperation among kin is the leitmotif.
It's been quite a long time
since I've seen you
and may be equally
this length of time
again.

> The slipping away of sand
> almost indiscernible
> unless the home
> is perched on the cliff
> overlooking the ocean
> waiting to be inundated.

navigating our concretised cognitions
so many pieces to the puzzle
sound and meaning
abstract domains...
don't take it too far
circularity needs to know only
when does the answer emerge?

Expectations and common sense
turns out not to be
so common.

                    Externalizing language
                    by closing your eyes
                    embracing the cool, calm air
                    and envisioning you there
                    it is the subtle scenes
                    the footfalls, the coughing
                    That, I yearn for just one day.

"How do you extract a poison
from a plant and prepare it
to put it on an arrowhead?"
you once asked me.
Well, you need the nimbleness of mind
and sophistication of thought
the secret is
knowing what to ignore
and what plant
you ought to seduce.

An Onanist's Creed

Roger Venn*

Slip
    that
        one
            past
                the
                    censor's
                        punctilious
                            pen;
                                is
                          the
                      mulberry
                plum
           pomegranate
    mauve
flute
    the
      deeply
          amaranthine
                scabbard
                  fleshy
                    firmaments
                        firmly
                    felt
                in

a
fashion
like
the
feverish
fornatrix
feloniously
fossicking
through
fever-dream
fantasies
of
exultant
finales.
That
Violaceous
periwinkle
purse
home
of
disappearing
dreams
of
genealogical
surcease
spilt
on
work-a-day agricultural carpeting.

Mixed Messages, Bro!
Name supplied.

Talk me through this one, bro

The Confederation of the United Northern Tribes

flag of independence 1835, unceded, āe, ka whakamāramatia

Tino Rangitiratanga ensign, ka whakaaetia hoki

the Stars and Stripes, well, ok

the Ban 1080 placards, ok, each to their own, at least there is a

scientific debate, but the one that needs explanation

is the tattered Trump 2020 flag fluttering on your porch

when his connection to environmentalism and indigenous

rights

is tenuous at best; evidence is he is climate change denier,

runs roughshod of indigenous rights; is a staunch opponent

of democratic values; fomenter of the attempted Jan 6th

insurrection; exhorting conspirators in Washington, DC to

violence and unable to accept a clear electoral defeat; of

encouraging hatred for his own Vice-President

(a man who himself was a great enabler, but no politician

deserves hanging for doing constitutional duty); there is a lot

of conspiracies to make this one even close to believable.

You've backed the wrong horse, bro, it is a lame donkey. All hail the Great Liar -in -Chief, Te Tangiweto nui. History recalls the 45th President of the USA, not as as a victim, [*pleeease*] but before, during and after his Presidency, incontrovertible evidence has as a victimiser. You've been hoodwinked, bro! Bizarre, why anyone in Aotearoa looks to the Great Self-Aggrandiser for guidance and leadership beggars disbelief. The ultimate fake newser for the 'alternative "facts"' crowd. Bro, this guy is no friend of indigenous peoples; no friend of respecting the rule of law and democratic principles; heading for multiple indictments--not because he is a threat but simply because he is a crook, and the smoke and mirrors Trump 'empire' will collapse like a house of cards. Why are so many craven Republicans afraid to see the self-evident truth? Bro, we don't need to look to the United States for inspiration-- plenty of good Māori, Pākehā and Tauiwi mā we can call upon even if it is fashionable to whinge and moan without offering solutions in the slipstream of COVID. Choose your delusions carefully, bro, Let's not praise te Tangiweto nunui o Amerika or invoke his ultra-right neo-conservatism here bro; Trump is no friend of Māori, Pākehā or Aotearoa. Ka pai though Dude, I guess that makes you a maverick or a renegade or an attention seeker, ka nui te pai; there must be some arcane reason you fly that flag, but I confess bro, you've got me stumped!

Kia tūpato! Kia mataara! Āta pānuitia

Kimihia ngā mahi rangahau motuhake

Ka tapatorutia te huinga o ngā puna mātauranga rerekē

Kia mau ki te ngākau tūwhera me te whai i ngā wāhi e puta ai

ngā taunakitanga (kaore i ngā whakapae)

Whakakahoretia ngā kōrero nenekara kē[44]

TE HUNGA RIRIKI

TE KOHANGA REO

---

[44] EDITORS NOTE: Translation of Te reo Māori text: Be careful, be vigilante/ read diligently/seek out independent research/triangulate different sources of information/ Maintain an open and follow credible evidence not just suppositions/Reject illogical foreign notions. [The author does not purport to represent te Kōhanga but supplied the image as a political response.]

Te Hunga Ririki Te Kōhanga Reo

Te Ingomuna

Kind people have a wonderful dream
make the dream real.
In the not-too-distant future
every child would enrol in Te Kōhanga Reo
to make good on the promise of Te Tiriti
that every child is bilingual
has the full inheritance Te Tiriti imagined.

Tāngata atawhai, me moemoeā whakamīharo
whakatūturuhia te moemoeā
i te hekenga mai o anamata, e kore e tawhiti atu
kia whakauru ia tamaiti ki Te Kōhanga Reo
kia pai ai te kupu oati o Te Tiriti[45]

> KO TENEI TE PAPATAKARO MO NGA TAMARIKI O TE
> HUNGA RIRIKI TE KOHANGA REO,ME
> TE WAIROA-ITI MARAE.
> THIS PLAYGROUND IS FOR THE CHILDREN OF TE
> HUNGA RIRIKI TE KOHANGA REO AND
> TE WAIROA-ITI MARAE.

---

45 The Author does not necessarily represent the views of
Te Hunga Ririka but includes the image as a refection of a
bilingual, tāngata Tiriti nation.

Groundswell of Incomprehensibility
Trevor M. Landers

Groundswell protest, Trevor Landes (2022)

What a plonker!

Disrupted climate, means no farming either.

Do you want your children to be growing pineapples and bananas, or farming land that cannot support your current activities? If so do nothing, and help condemn everyone into the bargain. Or act responsibility; and strive to maintain a way of life. You have a choice! No one is out to eradicate farmers, but behaviour change is needed across all sectors of society. Simple as that.

Floods, droughts, environmental havoc, greater climate instability. Do you watch or read the news? Who was in He Waka Eke Noa? Farmers and their representatives were there in force. Consultation is not the finalised policy. Do you understand democratic processes? My guess is existing significant mitigation and carbon sequestration will be included. Is this your first dalliance with such processes? You seem woefully naïve.

You won't always get what you want, but spitting the dummy is the response of the Luddite, and those lessons are worth learning. As a farmer's son, you are besmirching responsible farmers and sullying a sector with the wacky manure you are spreading, and your passive-aggressive vigilantism. Do you fully understand the scale and complexity of the issues? I ask because I am genuinely curious.

Climate change mitigation will make the COVID pandemic look like a Christmas Party and we are virulent variant away from more disruption. That is science, not guesswork. Not easily digestible but scientifically certain no matter how much you dismiss, discredit, or ignore the climate evidence. And why would clever farmers do that, anyway?

Farmers are arguably the most invested and most threatened by climate change, yet Ground stall antics again suggest they really don't understand the nuances or complexity and are simply wide-boys in tractors who like to whinge and moan on the basis of misinformation and being unaccountable for their actions.

Just play your part, pay your fair share. No more, no less.

Polluter pays. With the exception of biogenic methane, the

solutions largely involves changed farmer behaviour. Smart farmers will pay less, clueless ones who do not change will pay more. Is that why their opprobrium bristles with fury? Agricultural Darwinism perhaps? I would never be that unkind, but today a small segment of farmers makes dicks of themselves and did damage to the rural sector at large into the bargain.

The days of doing what we have always done are over for all of us; most farmers appreciated this long before the latest groundswell of incomprehensibility. Consumers in our trading partners are already looking at us. We could lead the world, if only those like Groundswell would wake up and see they are sabotaging the very industry they purport to support. Do you really think trading partners won't monetise good responses to climate by a country's agricultural sector in future? They will!

Sheesh, wise up buttercup. Taxpayers have carried agricultural emissions for long enough, and thankfully entry in the ETS is coming in 2025. It will penalise muddling Neanderthals and the misinformed minority peddling falsehoods and fear-mongering most because they will not change and they will be penalised. Most farmers (and their children) care deeply about the land. Groundswell thinking is antiquated, and quaintly anachronistic and laughably simplistic. It engenders pity, compassion and mirth.

We, the citizens of the world are failing the planet, folks. All OECD countries are tracking to exceed the 2% target by some distance, which sets climate change into acceleration mode. What is so difficult to understand? Farmers have been

outside the ETS for years; that the climate catastrophe has started to unfold is undeniable; and some want to bury their heads in the sand, but most will change behaviour and play their part. Farmers, those in coastal areas, and industry where flooding/drought will intensify, will be bear the brunt of rises in temperature, and more erratic, cataclysmic weather,

Yet Groundswell comes to towns and cities in new long wheelbase Utes and expensive diesel tractors never once self-reflexively seeing the idiocy and the bitter irony of your behaviour today. What kind of world do you want to leave to the next generation?

'Over-simplifications to the point of absolute absurdity'© Trevor M. Landers, 20 October 2022 (both photos).

Homages to Waitōtara

Matawai

Apirana Taylor

Taranaki, what does that word mean and
why should it mean a thing to me
far removed from my roots I survive
voices from days not long past whisper
stirring leaves in the wind
a murmuring of birds
hunger for land, home fires
Taranaki, Maunga rongo
my heart beats aueee...
te mamae, ngā matawai
o Taranaki
to the tears of the
mountain i will go
my bones live there

Signs of a Homecoming

Anonymous

The sign is near Pakaraka Road
an artificial divide
     Farewell Whanganui, Kia ora anō Taranaki!
But there are
  alternative ways of knowing, seeing
     the rohe of Ngaa Raaru Kiitahi
does not recognise such arbitrary demarcations.
  Did you ever notice Te awa Waitōtara as you
    careened down the big dipper
      crossing the bridge to hoon it up
  a serpentine passing lane?
     Faster, faster, pussycat
and *damn the torpedoes, skipper*! So hoofing
  it into Taranaki like *Operation Barbarossa*
    strapped to an internally combustible engine.
  Roared past Waitōtara, didn't you?
     As if it wasn't really there.
   Oh, but it is: defiantly, proudly, & curmudgeonly stoic.
Not just locals swilling, or an eke'd existence
  but a world oft undiscovered
    a rich pageant; daily indomitabilities of spirit
   remember this as you hurry onward to:
  Weraroa | Wairoaiti | Waverley

    & deeper into the heart of a homecoming.

spring rain
Mike Oliver Johnson

spring rain gladdens the earth

celery and stars grow fat

dark earth roots, tangled

the gallant Sweet William

the passion of pink primula

blood's fitful shaking

heart searches for home

among the trails to snail heaven

love in the airways, love in the byways

we sprinkle white shells on the path

to look pretty

and for the night folk to find their way

a touch tell us the shape beneath

the moist swell of the garden

a word returns us to the starting place

the opening place

the morning's first tūī

dazed flowers bloom in the dark
turn this way and that
through the four directions
searching for the sun

as I fall apart, I fall together
resurrected in every step
never thought I'd get this far
never expected it to happen

I might have stayed asleep
not bothered to wake up
if the sky hadn't touched me

that tin-tin-nab-u-lation on the tin roof
is a ghost rain, a fairy rain, a rain
arriving from yesterday
having lost its way
found again on your wet lips

The Waitōtara River

Trevor M. Landers

We marvel
   at the birds defying gravity
hovering supernaturally
   in the buffet of onshore winds
like clothes on a line
    determination into the teeth of it
      kudos to you, ngā manu rere-tere

Across the still Waitōtara
   that are no flumed logs
shrieks and squawks
   of a competitive airborne armada
it is a shitty old business
    someone has not fenced their riparian margin
      some fool
      thinks a river is a lavatory
      in 2022: a disgrace.

Not many edible fish here, e hoa
  try the fish fry at the Hotel;
    the brown river

no holiday condominiums for swift fins
washed & drained & sedimented hill country
    volumized to near complete black tea opaqueness
    (another inglorious story of a tannined, silted
    New Zealand river, quite unnecessarily)
    headwaters muddied by land clearances.

In the slow, awkward limp of rehabilitations
    old man river waits for a hip replacement
staggers onward, incontinent towards the sea.
One day, hopefully, our mokopuna
    will look at this river
    with respect for what it gives,
    the kai, the soul of the whenua
  but we will be in our graves
    & I hope that have no reason to curse
    our inertia and indifference
    we see more interested in deflection
    than fronting up,
    and addressing it squarely.

Te awa o Waitōtara ki Makakaho Junction © Trevor M. Landers, (October 2021).

Te Awa o Waitōtara

nā Te Tuhi Holdsworthy me Trevor M. Landers

Ka hipa koe i te kura paurauri
    erangi e kore e mahea ake
     whai muri i te whare patu o Waitōtara
erangi tonu ki te hoki ki pūkaki o te awa
     Ka kitea tō awaawa, ka mahea ake tō rerenga hoki
kāore he para ki te puna.

You pass the school brown
   and you don't get clearer
     after the Waitōtara slaughterhouse
but up river, you flow clear, your riverbed
no silt and rubbish at the source.

Camping out the back of Mangawhio

Michael J. Back, with Trevor M. Landers

Long drive
hefty hike
      Omata Valley
      perfect place
            campsite secure
            erection follows
                  billowing tent
                  staked down
            relax inside
            German lager
      chicken chips
      hummus dips
sleeping bags
kerosene lamp
      telling tales
      laughter loud
            tall stories
            past glories
                  snoring loud
                  farting proud

        restless legs

        persistent rain

    grim insomnia

    exhaustion plain

wind rush

manuka-kanuka

     Morrissey wails

     spirits sink

         Thom warbles

         much better

             thunderclap

             torrential rain

        mouths dry

        muscles ache

     early sunrise

     bleary eyes

tent flaps

open wide

     new day

     perfectly clear

        moving on

        tramp further

            glorious bush

            for two mates.

History as the very soil beneath your feet
Paul Davies

You ask about the colour of history, and I can only reply drive

a dull shovel into the rich loamy earth,

sing to you in the broken melodies of suffering. Still,

I am moonstrong, held in a god-hand, fused and positivity of

a brighter future,

a petition, a protest, a Treaty settlement,

the future

has arrived, if we care to grasp it.

I have milked cows around Waitōtara,

there is CausMag

in my diaphragm

    and fescue seed around my nostrils.

Rucksack and Redbands at the ready.

In the aubergine moonlight,

    loam gleams, grasses at the zenith of green. I hear voices

more than a hundred years old,

Bloodied my fingers, store DNA beneath my nails for a
purpose
    I cannot discern

I sleep with a wide bay window open.
   I love the song of the rūrū,
      the karaoke of tūī,
        the kererū heavily laden in flight
the plump-breasted flutter
   gentle grace of Kārearea
     Part of our whānau too.

No man should live with an alibi
   take the grievance of the past
      to propel the present.
Learn---understand, work together
     a cell for the language of rancour bones to make perfect
     the reconciliation
their story, family, a bedroom pact
   & now, this soil can be ours to tend
     for the whole term of a life.

Makakaho Junction © Trevor M Landers (2021).

That Weekend at Makakaho Junction
Name Withheld

That weekend

imprinted on my skin

when our bodies fused

and passion was only currency

That weekend

is seared on my mind

a co-mingling of arms and legs

a commonwealth of fucking and want

That weekend

still pervades my tongue

the dewy sap of you never so sweet

time bouncing from orgasm to orgasm

That weekend

the clandestine venue

like a deluge for twin desert shores

I wear in my heart

with

pride

and

lust.

The Great Waitōtara Drought: A Pastoral

Trevor M. Landers

Summers' tang emulsified to desiccant juice
powdered falls, this searching sunlight searing
the new unpeaceable solar rain, the language of rainlessness.
Trees and shrubs accented, assuming new
brogues in chalky mouths, no elephant-bodied clouds
stampeding across the sky, hoggets bleat, mewling at
denuded hilltop fortresses, shorn of all leafy palisades weeks
ago.
Between coming, arriving, and detours onto the secondary
roads pot-holed and pock-marked by Fonterra tankers
and old tractors
matted, rotting roadkill becoming a road ornamentation
pelt and asphalt a new viscid fibre
dusted by a cavalcade of a thousand ute rides
the odd round bailer and farm implement
air so thin that the act of breathing perforates it
a membrane opening up, sucked back like a bubble, into a
cud; a new code for sparrowed powerline semaphores
the murmur creeping from tree unto tree
sorry, fella, still dry, mate.
Hairpin blindside,

the Ute has right away in case of two utes astride, the smaller

yields; muscular driving interpretations here, Jimmy, the road

we drive has no apparent outcome

not wrongly taken, just meandered down in a leisurely way

that will soon earn disfavour become a historical footnote in

human transportation.

The listless trees languidly overhang perfect for a leigh shade

for a moment; an obsolete creek nearby took up, running,

disappeared in the clamour of cicadas.

The kingfisher divines water from the compact & stony ground

two giant hares, sentries, pan the paddock for speck of green

the farmer's dog off the leash, slim pickings either way.

In the back of the car,

a bottle of Lemon and Paeroa is passed to me

to the parched and slack-jawed

manna from heaven underneath the Macrocarpas.

In a faraway paddock, cows bellowing, spotting us,

the ruse is up,

we have not come bearing any gifts

not even a cob of maize or wild turnips

or anything that holds the memory of water

like a benign grandfather

lovingly remembered.

The Elemental Poem: The Rain at Ngāmatapouri

Trevor M Landers

Full disclosure, I know the history, wound my way up twice, first time, summer, cracking sunshine, forest was steamy; great walk. Second time, road was slushy, plenty of slips, raining like Norway. This poem commemorates the second visit: 47kms of wind, wend and wound in whistling wettenstance.

There, your wind with its battering banter eroding hills creating slippage, downing telegraph wires, thussocking but we shall not be conquered, rain, our pluck is dri-az-bone. The church and the Rugby Club do not flinch, thrumped by gales, neither shall we! I will wager our obduracy and cunning, spin dice against your persistence, gratuitous use of force, gnarly insurgency typhoon-tempest we banish thee, move off this meteorological map!

One note rain, your looming downpour does not quake us, rain squalls swoop like demented hawks onto an Audi bonnet. Keep your melodic drumming for the roof, impertinent rain. Through surgically cut escarpments, the hills yield, orangery innards.

There are brown, baptismal pools on the road now, squishy cisterns. Not yaqona at all, brackish welcome mat of rain, opaque & bemired. You are a most mercurial guest, dancing to his own gumboot tango I pit myself against your juggernaut, floods of awe, angry whistling.

Downpour in Ngāmatapouri. Torrential does not even encapsulate you. Large globules of rain, gloop into sheltering foliage, globs and glebes. There is impasse, shelter bend, two statuesque Matai trees, respite! Road, now Lake Ngāmatapouri, festooned with debris, mud-slaloms.

As Monsoonal tide abates, rivulets carry water backward, draining, innumerable, small, small waterfalls languidly regressing. A true squelchy quagmire, we walk on defiantly, only 1 night lost, dry and warm. Leave unbowed but awestruck, planned visit No.3, a summertime fling.[46]

---

[46] An elemental poem simply conjures the elements or chronicles the interplay between meteorology and humankind. It may contain onamatapoeia but attempts to vividly transport the reader to the scene described. A very common genre of poem. This was first published in www.matatuhitaranaki.ac.nz

The zen of hiking out the back of Orangimea

Trevor M. Landers

Though the first carried more miles,
the second day of the hike was totally and
unapologetically

 l
  l
 i
 h
 p
u

 When you ascend, hiking becomes the zen
of endurance
before then:
   sinewy st re tc hi ng
muscular b_u_r_n_s.
First, you are stripped
 of all the pleasures of hiking
  excitement rendered down to lactic acid
  baked and hardened trail
captured by a reverie—the pyrrhic dream of moisture.
The oppressive sun shrivelling all underneath
 this thinning canopy

the tramper is unconscious, a raisin on a pillow.

A rare face, strangers passing you on the downhill stride---
only see your 'Please God Help Me' or that ominous knowing
smile,

slightly sadistic, full schadenfreude, grinning eyes.

eight straight miles under chaffing hell

60-pound pack under unrelenting sun

Each glade and colonnade, a brief respite

A zephyr is a new nirvana

you will long for the sweat and the torture that forces your
mind into calf-high mountainous terrain.

Homage to the deep valley behind and below you,

the past disappearing into stands of tawa and rātā

the bloody nimble goats, and blessedly quiet wild pigs.

The worst thing you can do is ignore pain—that makes it
relentless.

Instead, focus on the pain until you become it.

The only thing left is the moment between each step when
you remember why you are here and what it is worth.

Just the next step, and another. Every time your foot touches
dry dirt, it feels like it left twice the footprint, summoning a
footfall out of a shuffle.

Tramper's palsy, or Orangimea knees, he calls it.

Here is the intrepid rambler's wilderness.

One day, when your thighs are too weak and fettucine

your body will no longer table your pack, but

memories will fill it with such buoyant heroics no cartography
will dare call it a truth.

      All the pleasures and joys of the trail that you
once thought dissipated
   in the steam of uphill toil:

Up

     up

       up

       will come rushing back
with the magnified strength of every year between you
     and the present
       you once knew:
  down
     down
       down
        down

the rabbit holes
the possum bivouacs
the tombs of fallen trees
the carcass of a long-lost sheep
past

past
past
the out of place spikes of gorse
the pretty but noxious ragwort
a wasp nest deserted by its sentries
the brusque caress of manuka
the stubbornness of tussock

Names like:
Mouhamaki,
Mangawhio
and Weraweraonga
emblazoned on your internal organs
like burnt wood fretwork
This shall not be a dull memory of pain, dark,
sombre and incomplete
the years past making it a Stalinesque triumph
replete with coronation
and a celebratory beer
near enough to the summit
& more foolish resolutions than a 5 Year Plan.

Underneath the old railway bridge on the Waitōtara River with Kathy

Name Withheld[47]

A bridge over the Waitōtara Mātātuhi Taranaki (2023)

In those days

my sandwiches

were the highlight of my school day

---

[47]Pseudonyms have been used to protect personal privacy. Kathy Bell is a pseudonym for a real person.

(luncheon sausage, vegemite and cheese).

In Standard Six, I would gaze longingly

at the classroom clock for 3pm, the bell rung,

a new adventure with Kathy Bell* on our bikes

biking through town, racing along

my cheeks bright red with embarrassment

and we would reach the river

leave our bikes in the long grass

duck under the bridge

trade un-eaten items from our lunchboxes

swap drink bottles or throw stones into the river.

It was there where I mustered all my courage

to tell Kathy I liked her

and she knew what kind of 'like' it was,

and in response she kissed me on the cheek

and my face was hot and beetroot red but blissful

I hadn't thought about her saying yes, you see

& more kisses under the bridge

lingered long in the memory.

At Waiinu Beach

P.J. Schaeffer

At Waiinu Beach

   before we head off for a wander

      we stop and have a drink

since the obvious invitation existed

    hospitality embodied in your hips.

        the tide is coming in; it is a metaphor

the earth's once molten crust

   exposed for critical examinations

A balatron waffles about fishing

    unless he too is speaking in metaphors

      our interest remains risible

before a treatise on laughability compels us to explanation:

    we have come to unfurl ourselves

      so have the decency to stop talking, man.

Kaua e Momi Haurehu ki te kura o Ngamatapouri

Trevor M Landers

Kaua e momi haurehu ki te kura o Ngamatapouri, he pai ake te hau māori ki a mātou, koinei te kōrero o ngā tamariki i kōnei.

Kei te ngana āhau ki te whai whakaaro mō ngā tamariki me te kaiako e momi haurehu ana tata ki te kura.

I tino kataina āhau. Ko te mahi o ētahi o ngā āpiha tūturu o te Manatū Hauora, ko te tuku kōrero ki ngā tamariki o te kura tuatahi mē tēnei kaupapa, te āhua pukuhohe.

From Oita-ken to a Waitōtara Bach, 2020: A Facebook Messenger Odyssey

Rachel Greenwood and Trevor M Landers

R: Takajolily reporting. Hāwera blown away, and Pātea deluged, quite the summer in Aotearoa. We are enjoying the flowers blossoming; a farrago of pretty floral bouquets pervade.

T: Fantastic! I hope you got the Noam Chomsky piece, 'History does not go in a straight line'. I know I am meant to be relaxing at the beach (the bach is lovely) but I couldn't resist as he is one of my favourite public intellectuals, noted for his insightful critics of American foreign policy and intelligence [sic]. Still, I am boring you probably. Flowers are much more alluring and affecting.

R: Yes, you can have the Belorussian Embassy send your completed passport to me in Oita. They are ridiculously strict about declarations and contents re EMS, so normal airmail might be better as the enforcement is not as stringent. Is your trip to Minsk related to your recently completed Master's on the historiography of Stalin in the West at UC?

T: Yep. And now, because of COVID, I have a tourist visa and a transit visa from Belarus, and they will both be forever elegant souvenirs in my passport. No donations to the Ukrainian and Russian legations thankfully. I hope you are enjoying the three bags of Snifter Lumps in payment for your postal and philatelic mission. Well deserved! Thanks! I know how special treats from Aotearoa can be!!

Innumerable games of 'Quiz Planet', an online general knowledge test. Rachel is a formidable opponent; Trevor is a titanic foe.

R: They're new on the market so I hadn't tried them yet. A crazy-bizarre mix of pineapple lump and snifters but it works! Hai! Japanese customer service is undeservedly famous and can be non-existent even in large organizations like the post office. You also get in trouble any time you go off-script or ask for anything unusual. AirNZ beats ANA in customer service at least... We have the second highest [COVID mortality] numbers! As of today, schools and some business closed, panic buying has begun. I'm not worried about the places; I'm worried they won't let me in!

T: Yes, Kiwis are shockingly complacent and dangerously smug. Italy, Spain, Japan, the United States could easily happen here though our geographical isolation is a massive advantage.

R: Just heard the Olympic Committee suggested deferring Tokyo 2020 to 2021. It really is all very unprecedented.[48]

---

[48] Actual and edited FB Messenger correspondence between Rachel and Trevor in 2020.

The Member of Parliament for Waitōtara

Trevor M. Landers

"There is a cult of ignorance .... and there has always been. The strain of anti-intellectualism has been a constant thread winding its way through our political and cultural life, nurtured by the false notion that democracy means that my ignorance is just as good as your knowledge."

- Isaac Asimov

The Hon. Venn Young. © Parliamentary Library Collection, c.1975

Only four members ever & aged 4, I met the man who

would was the 3rd, the Hon. Venn Young,[49]

the Member of Parliament for Waitōtara, probably a year

after his most controversial bill to legalise 'homosexual acts'

between consenting adults---the country was a conservative

bastion in 1975--- & to me he was a friendly towering

colossus of a man, avuncular yet overwhelming to a small

child.

He had played rugby against my father; they knew each

other pretty well. Venn himself donned the amber and black

with considerable aplomb, a bullocking No.8,

and both worn the blue rosette

like venerable old school conservatives:

fiscal prudence, social liberality---

(the cult of the reified self & avaricious neo-

liberalism had not infected the Nats gravely yet).

It was down to Venn, we got the pink volumes of Hansard in

---

[49] Venn Young was born in Stratford, Taranaki. He attended primary school in Stratford, but received his high school education in Nelson, at Nelson College from 1942 to 1944. He then returned to Taranaki, becoming a dairy farmer. He gained some distinction as a rugby player, representing Taranaki. He was also active in the Anglican Church. He was first elected to Parliament in the abolished seat of Egmont (1966-1978) before representing Waitōtara from 1979 until his retirement from politics in 1990 where he was succeeded by Waverley Pharmacist, Peter Gresham 1990-1993. The seat was abolished in 1993. Venn died in 1993, survived by his wive and nine children, including Jonathan who represented New Plymouth for the National Party 2008-2020. Venn was the Minister of Forestry, Minister of Lands, Minister for the Environment and Minister of Social Welfare (now Social Development).

the post—it was like Christmas to a boy!

I am sure, much to Dad's chagrin, the speeches of David

Lange offered glimmers of light under the yoke of R.D.

Muldoon.

There is a line of succession here too:

by no means a straight line, dear readers.

Bryce was the first, firebrand despoiler of Parihaka[50]

Hutcheson the second, canny lawyer[51]

---

[50] Bryce was initially the MP for Wanganui from 1871 serving to 1891 and was an infamous Minister of Native Affairs from 1879 to 1884. In his attitudes to Māori land questions, he favoured strict legal actions against Māori opposed to alienation, and he personally directed the invasion of Parihaka and the arrest of the leaders of the movement. Described as being stubborn and embittered to Māori Bryce was the public face of a harsh policy. When settlers were threatened by Māori led by Titikowaru in 1867, Bryce volunteered and became a lieutenant in the Kai-iwi Yeomanry Cavalry Volunteers. Bryce was proud of his commission, but an incident at William Handley's woolshed in November 1868 clouded his military career. Initially it was reported as an attack on a band of Hauhau warriors, killing two and wounding others and where Bryce was "prominent and set the men a gallant example" according to his commanding officer. Later reports had the Māori as a group of unarmed boys, aged from ten to twelve. As Chair of the Native Affairs Select Committee, He expanded the powers of the Native Land Court in order to facilitate the sale of Māori land, reduced the scope of the Native Department, and enforced the law against any Māori resisting land confiscation and sales. These actions made him deeply unpopular with Māori and Bishop Octavius Hadfield reported that West Coast Māori called him Bryce kohuru (Bryce the murderer).

[51] George Hutcheson was born in Scotland and emigrated to NZ with his family when he was 11. H represented the Waitōtara electorate from 1887, when he defeated Bryce, to 1893, and then Patea from 1893 to 1901, each time as an independent candidate. He stood aside for Bryce in 1883, but such was Bryce's unpopularity among even parochial supporters he was routed at the ballot box. George and his father were in Parliament at the same time and were often seen glaring at each other from opposite sides of the house. (His father held the City of Wellington electorate). Hutchison went to South Africa during 1899 as a legal adviser for Lord Roberts during the Second Boer War, and in 1901 the seat was declared vacant, and a by-election was held for a new seat of Pātea with redrawn boundaries. Frank Haisenden won as an independent but was soon dumped himself.

Gresham the last, Waverley accountant, Knight of Malta[52]

Our lounge hosted electorate meetings a youthful John

Banks and Winston Peters both came to stay at the farm;

Brian Talboys |Allan Highet |Ben Couch, Jim Bolger| & Hugh

Templeton all tucked into Mum's signature apricot muffins at

some stage.

    Not Rob; not one for jibber-jabber

      & greasing the wheel with small talk

   while a perfectly good hall awaited demagoguery.

Venn was that rare parliamentarian

      much loved, a man of the people

   not a political ideologue—a mind of his own

 'a decent joker', the heart of a lion.

Of the four, I must confess, he gets my vote by a very long

country mile.

---

[52] Peter Gresham was a Member of Parliament from 1990 to 1999. At the 1996 election, the bulk of his Waitōtara seat was merged with Whanganui to create the new seat of Whanganui, and Gresham was defeated by Jill Pettis of the Labour Party. Gresham remained in Parliament as a list MP, in the first MMP Parliament but retired at the 1999 election. From 1993 to 1996, he served as Minister of Social Welfare and Minister of Senior Citizens, a demanding and unpopular role given the 'Mother of All Budgets' Ruthanasia policies of Finance Minister Ruth Richardson that slashed benefit payments.

Veronishka (Waiinu Beach)

Tadeuz Ladowniki and Trevor M. Landers

How wanton this
body spreads over our afternoon

where I will travel daily
a student of history

between your long, inviting thighs
sensing the aroma of your arousal in the air

At Waiinu Beach, bikini-clad immaculate perfection
my eyes catch your warm embraces

I am the botanist in your garden
my surveyor's marker pegs bear down on you

the cartography of the amorous
nestled close, this is where my heart lies

in your rank, luxuriant bosom
I am open to the skies

Half-naked in soft, svelte ecstasies
so unashamed to lie, to gaze upward

& watch the heavens hurtle over us
I feel your lush arms enfolding me

pulling me inside
here is where I reside.

Eponymous house on Ngutuwera Rd, © Trevor M. Landers. (2021)

Dilapidated House on Ngutuwera Rd, Waitōtara

Trevor M. Landers

Dear Reader
    You may see the ramshackle exo-skeleton
a once-was-a-house reduced to an aesthetic eyesore
    the chancre in the grass, as if hobbled by gangrene
    the ultimate indignity, an opportunistic arsonist
but I do not see dereliction
    I see histories and stories secreted into admittedly flimsy walls
    grandeur of the disappearing past
    that people lived (and perhaps died) in this house
        lived lives of determination, joy and adversity
      as we all do in unequal measures
   not for fame, fanfare, but for fairness and aroha
To the collapsed roof, let me say to the lot of you
    we should all get old and suffer infirmities
to feel mysterious backaches, labour with painful hip
       now, job description changed,
   the tottering, tumble-down once-was-a-house
    on Ngutuwera Rd
      is simply transformed:
         a nursery for a family of thankful magpies, the plush
penthouse suite for a pre-eternally playful possum.

Not Just at Face Value: A Memorial Arch, Ngutuwera

Trevor M. Landers

Memorial Archway, Ngutuwera Road, © Trevor M Landers, (March 2022).

Driving down Ngutuwera Rd
    stumbling on a white memorial arch
        in remembrance of Willy Karipa,
            on the site of the old Waipapa Marae,
                (they moved it up the hill—incessant floods)

Willy, k-i-a, the Egyptian desert campaign.

The Desert Fox, Erwin Rommel & his Wehrmacht

a formidable foe

surviving the battle of first battle of Ruweisat Ridge,

an assault on Miteirya Ridge, fierce action at El Mreir,

but between the first stalemated battle of El Alamein, and the

watershed second, near El Alamein, 4 September 1942,

in the Matrouh Governorate

he died of his wounds

—the telegram no-one wanted;

the only son of Gunny-Gunny Karipa to enlist, lost.

Joined with his mates, missing the church service at Tutahi

before disembarkation, as if it was a portent

a superstitious tale without evidence:

(Davis and Katene also had the holey spirits

that night too; missed the service &

returned safely to their whānau).

We remember them.

The inscriptions sobering:

'Ihinga mātou mō te iwi. Hei konei'.
[We died for our people. Here we are].

Kia maumahara:

'*Kaore e aroha i rite ki tēnei i tuku i tōna tinana ki te mate [There is no greater love that to give one's life so that others might live abundantly].*[53]

Collective memories,

    so precious,

    long may they linger in

        the imaginative realm.

---

[53] Also commemorated on the back of the structure, Captain George Pokai, who died in Italy 1-6-44, Wi Wereta, who died El Alamein 26-10-44, and John Sullivan (Tatara Tieketahi) who served but survived the war. Thanks to Maureen Flutey (nee Karipa), Allan Davis, and Peter Luke for sharing their knowledge freely with me. Tēnā rawa atu koe e te whanau o Waipapa Marae, Waitōtara.

A Japanese-ish poem about the mural on the wall of the old Waitōtara Machinery Building

Amanda Fletcher

Stock standard

Taranakiana

mountain luminous,

azures, turquoises & cobalts

here

in

Waitōtara!

The mural on the Old Waitōtora Machinery Building © Mātātuki

Taranaki (2021)

Waitōtara Village Poem

Te Manea Gifkins, Harper Ferris & Noklair Milton

A tranquil peace

counting villagers

on hands and feet

Despite the floods

we have come back

in one piece: resilient.[54]

Waitōtara Senior School Children, July 2022

Trevor M. Landers

A school very like my own *alma mater*
Sacred Heart, Manaia, long since disestablished
but this one---the vim, the vibrancy, the verve
that unmistakeable rural primary atmosphere
pragmatics, practicality, candour and best:
a sense of pride, resilience and fortitude
kids wandering across SH3 from the village,
on bike or foot, or commonly the parental shuttle
from farms, from further afield
embracing novelty, taking on new experience easily
even today's new visitor and his poetical arc
and what a joy the three groups were
unleashing imaginations, the fanciful and fabula
working collaboratively like second nature
coming up with pieces adults would happily
plagiarise and claim suzerainty over all that is
uttered and all that is written.

Waitōtara School Reflection

Mekah Hayward, Coralee McClaren-Coe, Charlie Murphy, and Marcus Miller

Mrs Devane, a playful principal
Queen of Friday freedoms
admired by most, respected by all.

Mrs McAree, our teacher
always on the right track
shepherding our studies.

Rambunctious students,
Insane antics, like elephants
thundering down the corridor!

Pictured from L to R: Mekah Hayward, Coralee McClaren-Coe, Charlie Murphy, and Marcus Miller of Waitōtara School. Note the excellent diamante poems in the background which were not related to this project; Great to see these during our wonderful visit with talents children at an awesome country primary school. Our things to Principal Polly Devane and Mrs McAree and all the staff who make this visit so memorably unforgettable.

Image: © Trevor M. Landers, and Waitōtara School (July 2022).

A common occurrence

T.I.

Who amongst us
has not had a crush on a teacher
her gentle, reassuring manner
the faint scent of eau-de-cologne
or his masterful way
of never making us feel faintly absurd
when such a conclusion
seems both inescapable and unequivocal.
Those special teachers that touch us
believe in us
even when are assailed by doubt
and encourage and empower us
to imagine ourselves better and stronger

Over the Makakaho Junction Bridge to.....
T.I.

Imagine the pupils

who passed over this bridge on a bus

in Utes, on the back of a quad bike,

with mums and dads in cars,

or perhaps on a horse

or Shank's pony

to get their start in Ngamatapouri

and who now live in Pātea

Waitōtara, Whanganui,

Whangarei, Whangaparaoa, Wollongong

Wuhan, Warsaw, Washington DC, Worcester or Wurzburg!

Waitōtara at Matariki

Aeneas Thomson, Lachlan Mackintosh,
Mellissa Burnard, Honor Parsons, and
Regan Hawken (Waitōtara School)

Rural idyll near Ngātapouri and Makakaho Junction, © Trevor M Landers
October 2021.

Matariki twinkles in the sky

like shiny silver glitter

crushed eyes thrown in the night sky

they are the eyes of the gods

Behold the Māori New Year!

the shimmering Pleiades cluster

sparkling in the heavens

a herald of new beginnings.

From L to R, and B to F: Aeneas Thomson, Lachlan Mackintosh, Mellissa Burnard, Regan Hawken (front) Honor Parsons (front row) looking justifiably pleased as punch with their Matariki poem. Image © Trevor M. Landers and Waitōtara School, (July 2022).

Waitōtara before ANZAC Day

Anonymous

In every little place
those powdered by
juggernauts of war
find remembrance.

The red poppies
speak to the collective insanity
of manacled thinking
of those who decide war is sensible.

The gravestones
or white inscriptions
by those who don't actually
fight the wars themselves.

Let's wear the white poppy
to honour and glorify the peace
to keep that uppermost
to remove many causes of war.

In this district
the same as so many others
mother raised their sons
not for war, but for peace and happiness.

The war comes back you see
in hearts and minds
sometimes it cannot be shaken
we need memorials for their families too.

The Gun Emplacement at Waitōtora, source: Trevor M. Landers (2022)

The Waitōtara Anti-Aircraft Emplacement

Anonymous

We stand ready, Sir

two Vickers machine guns

a Bren gun

six Lee Enfield rifles

should any stray Messerschmidt 109e

or low-flying Mitsubishi Zero

enter our air space

we will strafe them with ack-ack

quicker than you can say:

Permission to speak, Captain Mannering.

The Foxhole

Anonymous

He is dug in alright,

like a real machine gunner's post

occupying strategic high ground

maximum visibility of his quarry

the same uniform

far from stand-issue

a jug of the amber ale

a Bacardi and coke chaser

prime spot this foxhole

directly in front of the rugby

smack bang in the public bar.

Porterhouse at the Waitōtara Hotel
Te Tuhi Holdsworthy

Masked up, my other half and I
    we are in for dinner, Porterhouse, and a Schnitzel
    a coterie of locals
    a troika of old farmer-types
swearing to beat a non-existent band
      creatively using fuck as noun, verb, adjective & adverb,
often in the same sentence, & the fisherman and foresters
seem to have eclipsed the farmers
    for best use of expletives in
      a comprehensible conversation for a fruity
        consonant-vowel ratio but the three
    black Labradors have heard it all before
      ennui fills their glazed amber eyes.
Only a Taranaki try rouses them momentarily
      bottles of beer in hand like a 1970s saloon
      testosterone palpable
      Mr Gupwell is grinning inanely
      Mr Davy is non-plussed
chuntering banter ricochets across the public bar

Potroz ghosts through a gap, sets up Blyde under the posts

folk wisdom is: Potroz shaving off his dreadlocks

has led to this good form, lead to the try

pretty far-fetched if you asked me but

that will be the beer talking....

Taranaki triumphs in the end,

unbeaten so far in 2021.

Final score: Taranaki 30, Otago 23,

the steak was very good too,

& we went unbeaten that year, is the footnote.

St Hilda in the Woods (Ngamatapouri)

Trevor M. Landers

Praise be the Canna Lilies

   the rickety barbed wire fence

   the impressively large red knocker on a wee postcard church

itself; for any assurgent modern Martin Luther figure charged

with reformatory zeal: the great schism of Christianity cleaving

the reformers against the sacerdotalism of the papists, that is

how, simply put, how this church came to be here. In 1517,

Luther's Ninety-five Theses or Disputation on the Power and

Efficacy of Indulgences, a list of propositions he railed against

abuse of the practice of Catholic clergy

   selling plenary indulgences; certificates believed to

     reduce temporal punishment in purgatory

      for sins committed by the purchasers or their loved ones,

the Pope's dipping into a vast 'treasury of merit'. A dissenter's

reward: Luther's ecclesiastical superiors tried him for heresy;

culminating in excommunication, 1521.But for us, St. Hilda of

Whitby[55]

---

[55] Hilda of Whitby or Hild of Whitby (c. 614–680) is a Christian saint and the
founding abbess of the monastery at Whitby, which was chosen as the venue
for the Synod of Whitby in 664. An important figure in the Christianisation of
England, she was abbess at several monasteries and recognised for the wisdom

near woods in Ngāmatapouri, who received the *viaticum* as part of the last rites, patron saint of

poetry, and the college that bears her name at Oxford University,

a pause, before the push on to Taumatatahi.

'Lilies at St. Hilda in the Woods' © Trevor M. Landers, October 2021.

---

that drew kings to her for advice.

The Ukrainian imbroglio reaches Taumatatahi

Volodymyr Shevchenko and Trevor M. Landers

Cartoon © Sharon Murdoch 2022

Voldymyr says

this valley is like nothing he has seen

Trevor says

most people in Taranaki have not even seen it

furrows of astonishment

etch themselves in a forehead

the car falls into silence

aside from *The Smiths* track playing,

Volodymyr starts to whistle to it jauntily.

We tootle on to Ngāmatapouri

desperately looking for a toilet now

so we head to the school

and commandeer a cubicle for two minutes

admiring the flower garden before the ride north.

We park before the road ends

we meet some pig and goat hunters

with rifles slung over their shoulders

who update us on conditions,

eventually expressing contempt for Putin

when the subject turns to Ukraine

this peaceful valley

the scene of a bitter denunciations

the gorse flowers profusely

even here, Russian iniquity is palpably obvious

once back in the car

Voldymyr says: 'you are good people'.

The Kaimoko and Mahema erasure

Joseph and Sophia Haddow

you will remember,
we agreed to make the venture together.
we should have been wiser to select a
section instead of in the hilly country up the Waitōtara River.
All we had to equip us for the job were youth, courage
and industry,
that made unmerciful demands
I need not describe the Ngamatapouri land.
It is all rough forest and hills, so rough that the tree roots rot
after the burn and the soil slips away leaving heart breaking,
ugly blotches of bare papa rock.
The fight with the returning bush is continuous
The greatest menace and destructor of pasture
has been the bracken fern,
but the Manuka is a close competitor in the ruin.
How long the struggle will persist nobody can guess;
to make farms out of such a surface
was heart breaking.
if our hearts didn't break it was only because
they were unbreakable.
[Sophia] hardly knew
a cow from a bull
and didn't know where the steer came on the scene

at all.

Ewes, wethers, rams, and hoggets were all just 'sheep',

grasses had no distinction one from another,
nor from grassland weeds either.

We are in the heart of the bush,

the road for wheeled traffic ended seven miles away and
beyond that for six more miles the road

climbed some eighteen hundred or nineteen hundred
feet above the river, which it left at Kaimanuka.

It was not a hard life we lived,

if by hard we have in view, long and strenuous labour.

It was lonely and entirely without such
entertainment as one could not improvise for oneself. Places
of amusement were not for us.

Annoyances   might be defined as vexations
without blasphemy,

Small accidents often of necessity, gave
rise to great inconveniences.

Coming from a literary household into the silence of the
bush   the change to your mother
was of no small magnitude.

We did the best we could with our own
books, and we subscribed to *The Spectator* and to the *Times
Literary Supplement.*

turnips and cattle were not allowed to absorb all our
faculties,   a danger of mental atrophy,

This social pabulum is missing in the seclusion of the bush.

Imagining Ngamatapouri

Maarit Andrzejewski and Trevor M. Landers

Maarit:
You love to stretch and expand
pushing beyond past boundaries
challenging me beyond measure
This time I may be stymied.
minulla ei ole aavistustakaan
Kuka tai mikä Ngamatapouri on tai oli
mutta se kuulostaa ihanalta kielellä
vaikka sanottaisiin suomalaisella aksentilla
I have no idea
Who or what Ngamatapouri is or was
but it sounds lovely on the tongue
even when said with a Finnish accent.
Für meine deutsche Seite
Ngamatapouri klingt noch exotischer
vielleicht eine Umweltkommune
versteckt in einem Wald in Neuseeland
For my German side
Ngamatapouri sounds even more exotic
maybe an environmental commune
tucked away in a forest in New Zealand

Trevor:
Ngamatapouri es una localidad

4

7 kilómetros tierra adentro desde Waitōtara
una comunidad encantadora centrada alrededor de una escuela y
silvicultura y los niños allí son bastante especiales.

    Ngamatapouri is a locality

    47 kilometres inland from Waitōtara

    a charming community centred around a school and

    forestry and the children there are really rather special.

Șoferul de acolo urmează un râu

Maiestuoasa Waitōtara

Există, desigur, un club de rugby, naturală

O mulțime de copaci și escadroane de motociclete

    The drive there follows a river

    The majestic Waitōtara

    Naturally, there is a rugby club of course!

    Plenty of trees, and squadrons of motorbikes

Un de mes disques préférés

Est le tronçon de route entre Ngamatapouri et Taumatahi

où la route proprement dite s'arrête et où les chasseurs se promènent.

Mais j'aime m'asseoir à côté du calme et de la tranquillité de la rivière

Omuri. Formidable!

    One of my favourite drives, is the stretch of road

    between Ngamatapouri and Taumatahi, where the

    road proper stops, and hunters hike in. But I like to sit

    beside the stillness and tranquillity of the Omuri River.

    Wondrous![56]

---

[56] This poem reflects some of the languages Maarit and Trevor speak: Finnish, German, Spanish, Romanian and French respectively. Our aim was to write a multilingual poem which people could still understand easily.

Radio New Zealand News at 2 (Taumatatahi)

Evie Ashton and Trevor Landers

Under the stony, speckled hisses
    of loose gravel
we frantically fondle buttons on the radio
      all for the news at 2pm
   the faint pulse of the pips!
      Wandering static and lo, the faint
stentorian tones of Evie's voice:

'Finance Minister Grant Robertson announced today......'
  '..was killed when a truck and their motorcycle collided on SH3'
  'Preseidnet Zelensky has addressed the United Nations to....'
  '.... anti-mandate protest in the capital spiraling out of control.....
Political reporter Katie Scotcher reports.....'

   <silence in Taumatatahi>

E: Inside the booth
   Soft, close sound
stillness surrounds
all the voices here. Headphones on
...just read, interrogate the page- you'll lose.

focus: Be here, be crisp, clear diction

   try not to stumble, gal

      avid listeners from Takapaukura? to Taumatatahi?

Are you there?

      Are you listening from Motupōhue to Manaia?

Bugger!

   The signal dies a faraway death

   a snippet falls in the gullies

      now, we are alone, removed of radio comfort

   a cruel and unusual punishment--Taumatatahi lagoon

         & we missed the bloody sports news too!

We pick it up again far south of Ngāmatapouri

      Radio New Zealand streams into the car again

         the Republic of Taumatatahi lies far behind us

      the kahikitea, the tōtara, the rimu and radio silences.

The Motorbikes of Ngamatapouri

Angus Sherwood, Charlotte Thompson & Tyler Rumball

Annoyingly loud, zooming up hills
flying over jumps, smoothly drifting through the mud
constantly fishtailing up steep, slippery slopes.

Wet wheelies, airborne whips
'scrubbing' the tip of the jump
Sailing along steadily, 'stoppies' in the gravel.

Tyler and Angus love Moto-X
bike engines roaring to the brink of explosion
hearts racing, sunscreen streaming into their eyes.

Ubiquitous here—they come with a hint of danger
cartwheeling down the hill after a crash
praying it is not written off!

Tyler, Angus and Charlotte at Ngamatapouri School, 30 June 2022.
© Trevor M. Landers

star jumper
Mike Oliver Johnson

Rumi dreamed he became a frog
leaping from star to star
without raising a sweat
and breaking the shimmering surface of spacetime
with his bulbous eyes wide
he isn't the only one
the whole cosmos is filled with hopping frogs
frogs that hop in from other universes
even unhopping frogs
that leap backwards in time
he wakes full of regrets for being a man
with toenails and underpants
all that baggage and a dusty walk home
he can't even call himself a tadpole
with a shred of self-respect
no cosmos leaping for him
he can barely hop from the bed
to the door and from the door to the gate
it's all one foot in front of the other
while one gets left behind to drag up the rear
a far cry from star-leaping frogs

and a menagerie of other transformations

of which the poet can only dream

stones that turn into birds

as they skip across the inverted pond of the sky

and the chitter of the skylark

turning into the music of the spheres

and the invention of galaxies

that turn constellations into ripe fruit

all of these things and the cartwheeling music

are one and the same as Rumi himself

if he only could see he is the frog

his mind is the lily pad

and all he has to do is leap about

little wonder being a man hardly cuts the mustard

nice as it is to have warm blood and quickening affections his

life is like a turntable turning

in one direction playing one song only

following as predictably as lunch follows breakfast

and he finds himself sinking, sinking into the mire

into the mirror for he has forgotten how to leap

how to break the shimmering surface breathe

and to set his sights on the next star

Washout on Waitōtara Valley Road

The Paisley Collective

Washout on Waitōtora Valley Road, Mātātuhi Taranaki (2021)

A kink in the road
hook right, loop around a tree
flood-prone road
washout left
a small avalanche of debris
like judder bars for the Utes
slows them down momentarily
but this is transitory, evanescent.

There is a kink in the road
deviations under a hillock
a new chicane
when the straight route
compromised by inundations
waterlogged soil surrendering
inexorable pulls of gravity
the mysteries of fluid dynamics

There is a kink in the road
we follow the serpentine Waitōtara
wending & winding up the valley
there will be other twists & turns
less permanent and more forgettable
she sits contented in the passenger seat
the lustre of adventure sparking in her eyes
together we navigate these byways
while the whippet sleeps through it all.

Ngamatapouri dreaming

Mike Oliver Johnson and Trevor M. Landers

Poetry is just the evidence of life.
If your life is burning well,
poetry is just the ash—Leonard Cohen

1.

this past century

a travelling ledger of creditors and debtors

marched up the same unsealed road

parched and often confused

seeking fortune

off the beaten track.

2.

occupation touches fever

for which there is no vaccine

summer's sun still lights up the south

houses settle into the earth

eked out of virgin, primordial forest

Mataī and Rimu strain towards the heavens

Kārearea circling in, Kārearea circling out

3.

At Ngamatapouri

he lies beneath a Ngaio tree

and look up at its flowers

hiding amidst leaves like tiny white brides

barely noticeable

the shadows criss-cross him

the sun shyly kissing face

like an over-zealous grandmother.

4.

Even with a pillow

I don't envy the darting pīhoihoi

always on the hop

or the vigilant makipai

forever swooping

even against the sunset

behind a lattice work of karo & kānuka

or the mad kaireka

its endless chitter-chatter

still gently mocking all-comers.

Pearl

Michaela Stoneman

My precious pearl is wayward
out in the cruel world
I feel I've lost a significant tooth
a show-off molar that comes with smiles
the hole feels so massive when
probed with my tongues' tip.

Made from friction
blackest sand rubbing
product of grind and chafe
the ring was on my trowel hand
my loss discovered in the pitch
black night, pissing down.

For the brightest moment
radiant warmth inside like feelings
I'll feel when I find her again
full like the moon
precious in the dirty squall
I searched, praying to something.

Eyeballs scanning earth seeing
small irregular oyster-jewels
shapely orbs in the form of

rampant oxalis bulbs
thousands of fake jewels
reproducing while we sleep

Pearl wannabes.
impersonators, pretenders.
she's out there somewhere
rubbing shoulders with the worms
free of finger prisons

naked as the fullest moon

Omaru River, Taumatatahi © Trevor M. Landers, October 2021.

The Cocoa Constrictor (Omaru River)

Sam Landers

Within remote idleness,
snakes a cocoa constrictor,
twisting through wop-wop space
at Taumatatahi
foraging prey on forest base,
greenery & scent surrounding,
hints of allergy to match,
summer pollen to play,
upon another golden day.

Pastoral Scene near Makakaho Junction,© Trevor M. Landers, (October 2021).

The Ngamatapouri Rural Life Idyll

Trevor M. Landers

Easy to make assumptions
  the ubiquitous ute out the front
    frontages as green as all Ireland
      the unmistakeable spines, ridges and scale
     of Tuatara-like hills, scampering up-country
     to the genuine wilderness
    rather than a wee bit of remoteness
    forty-odd kilometres up the Valley
   in splendid isolation for a while
   imagine having to talk to people
 and the perils of patchy mobile coverage
 or mother of all indignities
  life without fast-fibre broadband
  and working in all weather
   the ancient art of animal husbandry
    keeping ewes, wethers, hoggets, rams
     & lambs safe from marauding bad weather
     torrential rains, hale, gale-force winds
    whistling down the valley like a locomotive
    every culvert a leap of faith over swollen river
  brown, the colour and consistency of half-dissolved
 Milo; add in some battens, some crumpled fences
fallen trees, stir into a quagmire. One way in, one way
out. Handle that jandal?
  It might
   be a Ngamatapouri
    rural idyll for you.

The Rugby at Ngamatapouri on Saturdays

Ryleigh Seruwalu, Lachie Thompson and Poseidon
Vokurivalu-Rope

At Settler's Domain

every Saturday is a test match

the whole of Ngamatapouri in attendance

Ryleigh and Poseidon are always there

a great place to meet our friends

and run around afterwards

The best thing

is the lolly scramble for children

during the half time break

The second-best thing

is the drain next to the scoreboard

slip, sliding until we are completely sodden!

Ryleigh, Lachie and Poseidon at Ngamatapouri School,
© Trevor M. Landers, 30 June 2022

Word-Drunk at Waitōtara Beach (after Neruda)
P.J Schaeffer and Trevor M. Landers

Drunk as skunk on benzene fumes

And your unlawful MDMA kisses,

your wet enticements of body

wedged between my own deliquescent flesh

as if there was a pier lined with sentimental flowers

or a mariachi band manifesting public ardours.

Feast then, guide it skilfully, let fingers find fat

the sweet blubber of this kind of seduction.

Over the sky's seeking rim

the stalled breath of day

hanging in the stolid air

like a helium balloon with small leak

at downfall, we are welded together

arc and entanglement together under blankets

smeared eyelids, glebe of lust, and eyebrows raised

and we can count the sound of decline

a triumphal declaration, then fast to slumber

we lie like *Peripetus or slugs,*

unused to intimate attentions and so as the sun rises

& a driftwood fire embers its last

the bitter taste of the Waitōtara river

still on our breath

my tongue is a spent salamander

your mouth, a cave of its own moistened delights

at times, I longed for a spade

to dig a ditch for us

to look up at the twinkling heavens

without speaking

nothing to define this in any way

Just let to be ours a moment longer

linger with me

like a pear in a bowl:

Packham, Beurre-Bosc, D'Anjou;

it matters not:

firm flesh

sweet juices

remember that at least.

Makakaho Junction re-imagined

Trevor M. Landers

These are the lips, powerful rudders
pushing through groves of kelp,
the girl's terrible, unsweetened taste
of the whole ocean, its fathoms: this is that taste.
— "That Mouth" by Adrienne Rich

Calloused fingertips

trace silhouettes of smooth,

contrasting milky-white thighs.

Navigate rounded hips

with familiar fascination.

Inhalations whisper of longing.

The breaths catch,

while fingers orchestrate

an exhaled symphony

of moans & whimpers.

writing poems inside

her with deft fingers.

Our story began with

her scream & ended

with her soul on my lips.

I craved her mouth, her hair.

Hunting for liquid measures

of her I hungered, famishment

the flavour of her skin, the ballet

of our interlocking tongues.

Kuchisabishii (Ngamatapouri)

Trevor M Landers

When you lack hunger

but you eat

because your mouth is lonely,

this is when I

discovered your tongue.

Supernumerary Phantom Limbs (Ngamatapouri)

Trevor M Landers

On the drive back to SH3

the front seat is conspicuous

your absence is the synaesthesia of travel

the forest just a chromaesthetic blur to me

pelting rain, a maudlin mid-winter misophony

all glitches in the neuro-matrix

a reminder of what was and now is not

but you cannot grieve for what is no longer there.

I No Wai

Name Withheld

Receational Water Qaulity Monitering © Mātātuhi Taranaki (2021)

Further down the Waitōtara River
the water is the colour of steeped tea
up-river, the denuded hills, slippage & erosion
deposit loams and soil sediments into the water
survive in that perilous soup kōkopu & īnanga

Down before the bridge and the Waitōtara School
The water is beyond sienna, umber, bister, cinnamon

or dark brick; deep henna, burnished mahogany,
nut-brown and turbid, almost the colour of burnt chocolate
the result of sedimentation; erosion, and rotting ponga.

Further down under the railway bridge; a different malady
unmistakeable signs of bovine encroachment.
the tell-tale proliferation of grasses near the water line
the highly probable signs of nitrogen leachates; milking
cows but killing fish; duffing the awa for profit accretion.

The awa meanders still, past the reeking abattoir to the sea
'Progress', a teleological nonsense, reaps a bitter harvest
but for the want of riparian planting, fencing & wetland
preservation, this river would be swimmable & healthy
and the intolerable environmental discharge is just lazy.

What inter-generational theft do we still perpetuate
While climate change deniers live only for today
Without thought of a despoiled, degraded tomorrow
That will be upon us and then cows will not help
all the regret & remorse does clean not up streams & rivers.

The Dutch Skinny-Dippers at Tapuarau Lagoon

Trevor M. Landers

In the bloated carcass

of another stonkingly hot summer

I arise from the inertia of an excuse

to take a walk, let the littoral air

pervade my jaded nostrils.

Some nights, I read

This summer it will be my friend Lauren's debut novel

Mila and The Bone Man[57]

But I am getting ahead of myself, another existential folly.

That parched summer

even the moana wept salty tears for the arid whenua

like an old lover singing the old serenades

in the effluvium of ozone,

the invigorations of the zephyr

the low, doleful, maudlin moaning of a receding tide

the crepitating midnight bonfires

---

[57] Lauren Roche, *Mila and The Bone Man*, Quentin Williams Publishing, Christchurch, (2022).

the galvanising euphorias of gleeful dawns

a nude swimmer embraced by the ocean

the body is mine.

History here means a history of storms

rushing the kōuka trees headlong for unspoken answers

the voice of the tangata whenua, muted by amnesia

the soporific slumber is wearing off.....

I half-wish my tūpuna were all spared their bitter trials

but maybe without, this wild impatience would leave me

I love the nights here. The inky blanket of te pō; ngā whetū.

The quiescence. The space for self-reflexivity. An old map for

this place shows taniwha, like Te Wheke but I dive in, rising

like faithfulness itself, preparation, the ocean, my pallbearers.

But that summer, I startled two blonde, Dutch tourists,

skin-dipping in Tapuarau Lagoon; odd when the Waitōtara

and the South Taranaki Bight both have the quality of

propinquity; and, undeniably, better swimmable qualities.

They see me wandering the paddocks, far from blanching, I

am beckoned to join the frivolities in the turbid shallows

the slightly brackish pool festooned with blond, buxom

nubility flashing unabashed confidence and candour; Europe

became an exotic destination again; no, not the nakedness---the spunk, the fearlessness, the intrepidity; the undeniable pluck.

Stranger, we chatted for about 20 minutes convivially; I never once asked what great aesthetic or recreational values prompted two 20+ students to swim naked in the Tapuarau lagoon. Such things require no explanations.

Bedankt meiden! Leef goed en voorspoedig![58]

---

[58] Trevor's rough translation from the Dutch: "Thanks girls! Live well and prosper!"

Am I Hana?

Name Withheld

Down on the awa, the mighty Waitōtara
I was raised in cowshit
& country-spun resourcefulness
And then I was schooled
not a miseducation too appear a maverick
but a solid grounding

at Victoria Uni I found my niche:
history, Māori Studies and sociology
a few choice theorists
check out that Faber, Durkheim and Habermas
it was here I found Mihaka, Awatere, Ranginui Walker
and the rest---wrote essays about the 'Māori radicals'
but they were not so radical, unless fighting social justice
is radical; unless you are used to having submissive natives
who knew their place, held their tongue
a bit like my own parents---I don't blame them though,
most of us live the lives of our times without challenging or-
thodoxies, or wrestling with the hegemonies of the ruling class,
where Marx says power is accreted
in order to control and disenfranchise.
History tells the tale. Tell me I am wrong.
Those like Hana Te Hemara, Hilda Halkyard, Eva Rickard
Atareta Poananga and Donna Awatere;
all had things to say and you know
I knew about Ngā Tamatoa: an august Rāwiri Paratene
a youthful Tame Iti without his wondrous Tūhoe Mataora
Hana herself; effete, confident of word, steely determination.
My greatest shame was not knowing Hana grew up near Muru
Raupatu marae & that she was a kind, erudite wāhine Māori from
the same soil of Taranaki; I only learnt this on a hikoi to
TSB Showplace on Devon St West, an exhibition and event,
Now I am Hana, and you can be too, if it be your will.

Thoughts of Makowhai Station from Childhood
Margaret Hand

In spring the sheep are driven over scrofulous hills
While there is still mud knee-deep in every shadow
And the wind's edge is sharpest in the tops
The sheep come up from the canyons
like burnished cumulus cloud.
They move slowly, wearily. They leave unnibbled
Not a low-growing leaf, not sliver of grass,
Not a flower. The billiard table is ready.

In the canyon the river crossings are muddied
before the wild gorse is a riot of yellow, pretty, noxious &
noisome
There are a hundred twisted trails on the way to the yards
fashioned from the dirty corrals, from the craggy hills
where they have fed and fattened over the winter
soon the clatter of trucks will trundle up the valley
lives ended at the abattoir for Sunday roast dinners.

I have seen them going up in December
in the dusty-churning summers, wethers and hoggets
to be crutched in the sauna of the shearing shed

when the shearer's combs buzz and sweat flows like beer
in rivulets down the face of every rouse-about
When Makowhai Station still a white cloud of brightness
Lifted high against the sky, when the wind is a sweet zephyr
there is only a haze of green around the poplars
You can see by looking slantwise, never directly,
the barking huntaways, imploring sheep and day's end
supper
I have seen the sheep move across the ridgeline
As if that hill was alive with 1000 or more sheep
thinking and behaving with a singular hive mind.

And I have seen the names of the shepherds scribbled
on the walls of the shearing shed
like the Sermons on the Mount, or an ovine Talmud.
On the hillsides the kanuka fights for their rootholds
in the black rocks, in the frozen lava, in the scars of erosion
these are the names of boys, carved here and written,
whose wits, they say, aren't fit for any other work,
or men whose minds are still the minds of children,
who do not desire anything more of living
than to lie in the glittering shadow of a poplar
to watch Romneys grazing contentedly
and the gaze upon the flock,
moving downward slowly,
sated and stupefied by grasslands.

Why the changes to History in the New Zealand Curriculum cannot come soon enough

Trevor M Landers

Your head may never have laid on a squab at Te Ihupuku
Kei te pai. Kaua e mānukanuka. Kaua e āwangawanga.

Have you rolled into Ngāti Waitōtara Hotel; pressed the flesh.
Me inu i ngā wā katoa. Kaua e inu me te taraiwa.

You should know the wonder and joys inside Waitōtara School
He tino utu nui te ako. Whāia i te mātauranga.

Leisurely drive up the valley; Ngamatapouri and Taumatatahi
He wheako ki te ao taiao. Mā ngā rākau e waiata ki a koe.

Let your ngākau rest at the great pool of Omuri
Whakanuia tō tinana, arohaina tō mouri

In Manaia there is a street, down the road a significant marae
Kia mōhio ki te hiranga o mua o te marae o Tauranga-a-Ika.

Hear Poi E, vow to understand what the words mean.
He waiata whakamīharo a Poi E,
ka whakaatu i te pai o nga mahi auaha

Next time you pass by Ototoka or Moturoa, dig deeper
Kei te huri noa te hitori i a tātou.
Ki te kore e mōhio ka kore e murua.

Out on Ngutuwera Rd, find monuments to sacrifice
Ko te hunga e wareware ana ki o rātou hītori
ka kanga ki te whakaora anō.

Spend an hour at Aotea Utanganui discovering local history
He rite te hītori ki te ora. Kī tonu i te whakaari, i te hīanga, i te
whakapae, i te tinihanga, i te whakaaro nui, i te pōauau hoki.

If you have never been welcomed onto a marae: Now is good!
Ko ngā tikanga Māori ka hanga i runga i te aroha, te manaakitanga ki

te manuhiri me te whakawhanaungatanga hoki.[59]

---

[59] AUTHOR'S NOTE: No translations are provided. Instead, find them for yourself and build your knowledge of Te reo Māori, a language which is only growing in significance for all who call Aotearoa home. An excellent online bilingual dictionary can be found at: https://maoridictionary.co.nz

Waipapa Marae kei runga i te puke

Nā Trevor M Landers

Ka puta i tēnei marae whakamīharo
ehara mai rānō tēnei marae noho ai
e tiro ana ki te mānia o Ngutuwera
te nākahi o Moumamahi awa iti
e wiri ana anō he kaikoi, ko te kaweau rānei
kei muri i te tirohanga atu,
te mokomoko o Waitōtara.
I kitea e au i te Rātapu tūtaki ai ngā tāngata whenua
te whaea hāpūpū ki runga i te huarahi
ka whakawāwāhinga te paraoa
ko wai i rewa i tōku whakaaro harakore,
me te whai wāhi ki te kōrero i ngā mahi tōrangapū
i te whare mīere.
hoki atu ki te marae, kei te haere ngā whakaritenga
ngā mahi whakatikatika iti ki te kīhini
ka peitahia, ka horoi, te hāruru hoki o te ngote pūehu
ngā mene whakahoahoa,ngā hononga, ngā tohu aroha
ka neke atu tēnei motokā hikohiko me te haumūmū
ka waiho ngā waka whakamīharo i runga i te marae ātea
karangatia ko te manaakitanga, ko te. whakawhanaungatanga,
te aroha ki te manuhiri, te aroha mō ngā tāngata katoa
Kātuarehe ēnei tāngata![60]

---

[60] I nukuhia te marae ki te wāhi o naiānei i muri i te waipuke nui i te wāhi
tāwhito o te mānia. (The marae was moved up to its current location after a
great flood inundated the old site on the plain). He tino rite ngā whiti e rua

Impromptu visit to Waipapa Marae

It turns out this wonderful marae
was not always perched up here
looking out over the Ngutuwera Plain
the serpentine Moumahahi Stream
wriggling like a sidewinder or a salamander
and behind out of sight, the lizard of the Waitōtara.
I found it on a Sunday and meet the locals
the blunt matriarch up the road who melted when she gauged
my innocent intent, and conferred, an opportunity to
riff on politics in the Beehive.
Back at the marae, preparations are taking place
Minor renovations to the kitchen.
a lick of paint, some cleaning, the drone of the vacuum
friendly smiles, connections made, a fond wave
this electric car moves away in total silence
leaving an impressive fleet of Utes on the marae ātea;
Call it manaakitanga and whakawhanaungatanga--
a love for the visitor, a love for all people,
these people are simply marvellous!

engari kaore i tuhia hei whakamāoritia i tuhia hei hono ai ngā whiti e rua, āna
ka maha ōna āhuatanga. (The two poems are very similar but are not written as
translations but two related poems sharing many similarities).

Hei poroporoaki: He mōteatea ki ā tātou

Nā Trevor M. Landers rātou ko Vaughan Rapatahana, ko Ngauru Rawiri.

Whakamahana e te āhua

Whakaakoako koia nā

Māramarama tō atarau

Rarongahia tō kitea

kanokōkō kanokawhe

Porotutuki te wā kōtiu atu

te takawaenga o te pāroretanga

Pānui mai koa i āhau

whiua atu te tauhuna hauā

Pirorehe whetewhete

He whānau hou tātou

Nā te kupu

Nā te atua e ora nei

e ū tonu nei

Ake, ake, ake

Amene

Our contributors:

Ruhansi Amarasinghe is a year 12 student at Pātea Area School who enjoys writing descriptive pieces. In the future she hopes to study medicine at Otago University.

Evie Ashton reads the evening news at RNZ. She's a seasoned broadcaster with a well-honed and playful feminist perspective. Currently Evie lives in Tāmaki Makaurau where she's developing a feminist fintech called Lucies that generates wealth for women. Evie has a Graduate Diploma in Psychology and a BA in Women's Studies.

Michael Back is a distant relation of one of the editors but insists his Mangawhio collaborative poem was selected on merit rather than nepotism. A keen tramper, Michael lives in Palmerston North.

Tony Beyer lives and writes in Taranaki. His print titles include *Anchor Stone* (2017) and *Friday Prayers* (2019), both from Cold Hub Press. Recent poems have appeared online in *Hamilton Stone Review*, *Otoliths* and *Tarot*.

Te Aniwā Braddock is an artist, jewellery maker, occasional poet and a mother. She lives near Ōpunakē and responded to an article in the Ōpunakē and Coastal News, never thinking of the editors was also at the gig in the Kākāramea Hall!

Gaenor Brown has been a Teaching Fellow at the University of Waikato since 2013. Prior to that she completed a Master of Education in Applied Theatre and Drama and is currently a PhD student there also. Gaenor enjoys travelling, live music and New Zealand's vibrant arts festivals.

Outside of work she is a keen reader, writer, fitness fan and a devotee of her mokopuna.

Aroha Broughton is an occasional writer and says she "belongs to that large iwi known as Ngāti Broughton!".

Tamszyn Broughton did not supply a biographical note.

Martyn Brown visited Pātea only once but as Australian living in New Zealand he understood the importance of the town to both Taranaki and New Zealand history. Sadly, Dr. Brown passed away in August 2022.

Pasha Clothier is an eighth-generation descendant of Tahitian tapa makers who settled on Hitiaurevareva in 1790, and then migrated to Nof'lk Island in 1856. Pasha is mahu -- the third gender and collaborates to create diverse creative works connected to her hybrid Polynesian world views. She has been exhibited or presented in 17 countries.

Rosalina Cook lives in the city of Santa Ana, El Salvador, where she works as a public nurse. She will never causally ask an editor what they are doing over email ever again because it may result in another poem!

Miley Davidson is a year 10 student at Pātea Area School that has a love for performing arts. She has previously been published in *Toitoi*, issue 24 with her poem "Outside". Her respect for the environment shines through.

David Denning is, despite what his poem might suggest, an avid fisherman. He rates the South Taranaki coast as his favourite fishing ground though he admits it can cut up rough from time to time.

Craig Foltz is a transplanted California, thriving in Taranaki. As a writer & visual artist, his work has appeared in numerous journals, anthologies & galleries. His collection of poetry *LOCALS ONLY* was published by Compound Press in 2020, and another volume is forthcoming. He has previously released two books with Ugly Duckling Presse. He currently lives and works in New Plymouth.

For My Wairua is the whāriki in which her work emerges from. It is a creative exploration of the nuances of life as a fat, indigenous Māori, and Pasifika Wāhine in Pātea, For My Wairua says she exists in a multitude of forms (physical, visual, written, digital) with the purpose of decolonising and de-centering the dominant discourse always at its core.

Amanda Fletcher is a Regional Sales Manager based in Whanganui. She was inspired to write her poem after reading an article about this book in a local newspaper and after stopping in near another Waitōtara landmark.

Naomi Fitzpatrick was born in Pātea and spent her early life in the district before moving away to Palmerston North for her studies. Later she was a civil servant and a rewarding recovery teacher and is now retired in Lower Hutt.

Ingrid Frengley-Vaipuna is better known by her students as 'Whaea Ingrid'. She is a former Deputy Principal of Pātea Area School and is presently Head of Department for English. She is a talented and accomplished writer as well as being an inspiring teacher for over 40 years.

Rachel Greenwood was educated at Hāwera High School and completed a Bachelor of Arts in History and Religious Studies. Subsequently, she taught English as a second language in Japan, where she met her husband. Their family home is in Oita, Kyushu. Oita hosted the All Blacks for 2019 RWC being roughly 2 hrs drive from Fukuoka, and 3hrs from Nagasaki. Rachel is now in Taranaki, as her daughter started school at NPGHSthis year.

Jah'Quasha Katene is a student at Pātea Area School. During their poetry workshop she had a hard time seeing that her poem was both amusing and contained rich sociological comment. Jah'Quasha can feel justly proud of her work. Kia kaha e kōtiro mīharo.

Joseph and Sophie Haddow lived at Taumatatahi (Kaimoku) from 1893 until 1906. In 1898 Joseph became the first teacher at Taumatatahi and Marohema Schools, teaching three days at one school and then the next three days at the other. This is a found erasure poem from his "We Two" that can be found in 'Early Settlers at Taumatahi' at www.waitotara.co.nz

Margaret Hand grew up in the Waitōtara Valley before marrying a dairy farmer and raising a family in Rongotea.

Jacqueline Högler is that rare gem: someone who left Toronto for Taranaki. She has written poetry for many years, and her most recent poems have been published in *Mātātuhi Taranaki: A bilingual journal of literature*. See: www.matatuhitaranaki.ac.nz

Te Tuhi Holdsworthy is the *nom de lêttrés* of a South Taranaki native who lives and works in Wellington but is intimately familiar with this region. He always writes under a pseudonym to protect is privacy and that of his whānau.

Kristan Horne is a native of Christchurch but has resided in Taranaki since 1980 and had a stint in San Marcos, Texas. She works for Te Whatu Ora-Taranaki as an intensive care specialist. Her poems have sporadically been published in: *Matatuhi Taranaki: A Bilingual Journal of Literature.*

Janet Hunt, writer, academic and graphic designer. She was born in Stratford, lived in Inglewood and has retired to New Plymouth. She is arguably best known as one of New Zealand's finest natural history authors, and her award-winning biography of Hone Tuwhare stands among our very best literary biographies. Professionally, Hunt initially worked as a primary and secondary teacher before lecturing in design, graphics and media at both the Auckland Institute of Technology and University of Auckland. She has also worked in publishing as a production editor.

Ashlee Hutton is a year 12 girl who attends Pātea Area School who enjoys writing creative stories. She wants to be a farmer on her family farm.

Marnie James is in Year 12 at PAS. When she leaves school, she wants to study interior design. Others describe her as quirky and charming, a claim she strenuously denies. [*Editors:* We have proof, Marnie!].

Mike Oliver Johnson is a distinguished novelist and an accomplished poet and helped especially the creative writing programmes at both the University of Auckland (with Witi Ihimaera and Stephanie Johnson) and later at Auckland University of Technology. His recent writing can be found at: www.lasaviapublishing.com

Gareth Kahui hails from Hāwera (Ngāruahine, Ngāti Ruanui, Taranaki Tūturu, Te Atiawa, and Te Rarawa) and might be remembered for performing a haka while covered in molasses at the 2017 New Zealand Petroleum conference in New Plymouth as a protest against environment despoliation. He has since become an ardent advocate for education, the environment and Te reo Māori as a result of a life-changing decision to study at Te Wānanga o Aotearoa in 2016. He has not looked back since.

Joseph Kalisa holds a Bachelor's Degree in clinical psychology from the University of Rwanda. He has recently completed a master's degree in Narrative Therapy & Community Work at the University of Melbourne.

Phil Kawana was born in Hāwera, with affiliations to Ngāruahine, Ngāti Ruanui, Ngāti Kahungungu and Ngāti Rangitane ki Wairarapa. He is a noted poet and short story writer, winning a number of national awards. He currently lives in Ohawe Beach.

John Kearns is a resident of Vauxhall, Dunedin, with an interest in the origins of names and places. His curiosity was piqued when he read an article in the *South Taranaki Star* about this book, and 'The Other Waverley' began the resultant product. He says he likes 'Waverley North'.

Rachael Kellogg grew up in South Taranaki and her writing has strong agricultural themes. Her poem in this anthology was very highly commended in the open poetry section of the 2013 Ronald Hugh Morrieson Literary Awards.

Kiri was educated at Pātea Area School and that is all she wished to convey.

Tadeusz Ladowniki did not expect to still be in New Zealand but his job as in the oil and gas industry and CoVID-19 has kept him in the province. A native of Warsaw, his first ever poems in English were recently published in Landers, T., (Ed.), *In a JIFF: Taranaki Poets response to the Jewish International Film Festival*, Te Perehi o Mātātuhi Taranaki, New Plymouth, (2021). His first time published in an English language literary journal was in Vol.1, No.2, (November 2021) of *Mātātuhi Taranaki*.

Raian Lal is an E-sports gamer and likes to play basketball. He likes to travel and go shopping. He likes to eat food and also make it too. He attends PAS.

Sam Landers hails from Kaupokonui and is currently a health sciences student at the University of Otago. He achieved success in the Ronald Hugh Morrieson Literary Words and several of his short stories have appeared in *Matatuhi Taranaki*.

Sonja Lawson has lived in Taranaki all her life and has been a writer since childhood. Her favourite subjects to write about are animals (especially horses) and real-life events. She loved writing stories until she got sick with Myalgic Encephalomyelitis (M.E) so she changed to writing poetry which she really enjoys.

Dennis Litchwark is a public servant for a Shire Council in greater Sydney. He has links to Pātea through his whānau who lived in the town when his family emigrated to Australia in 1982. He is mainly of Ngāti Ruanui and Ngāti Kōtarani descent but thinks there might be some Guernsey, Irish and Taranaki antecedents in the mix too. He describes his irregular writing as somewhere 'between being provocative and copping a right hook to the head'.

Kataraina Murray was in Year 12 at Pātea Area School. This is her first ever published work, She affiliates to Ngāti Ruanui and Ngāti Hauiti.

The **Ngāmatapouri School 'Poets Society'** comprises the following budding bards: Angus Sherwood, Charlotte Thompson, Tyler Rumball, Ryleigh Seruwalu, Lachie Thompson and Poseidon Vokurivalu-Rope.

Airana Ngarewa (Ngāti Ruanui) was born and raised in Pātea, and is a very talented writer. He teaches at Spotswood College and is studying a Master of Teaching and Education Leadership with Ako Mātātupu:

Teach First NZ. His writing has appeared in *Newsroom, Headland, Mayhem, Turbine, Takahē Huia Short Stories*, and *Mātātuhi Taranaki*, among others.

Dr Mikaela Nyman is a writer of poetry, fiction and non-fiction. She is the co-editor of *Sista, Stanap Strong! A Vanuatu Women's Anthology* (THWUP, 2021). Her novel *Sado* ('Shadow/ Shadows') was published by THWUP in 2020; her first poetry collection in Swedish *När vändkrets läggs mot vändkrets* (2019) was shortlisted for the Nordic Council Literature Prize 2020. Her essays can be found in *Ko Aotearoa Tātou | We Are New Zealand, Strong Words: The Best of the Landfall Essay Competition* #1 and #2. In 2021, she was the Massey University and Palmerston North City Writer in Residence.

Rosanne Oakes (née Reardon) was born and bred in Pātea and left to pursue a career in education. 30 years later she returned and held both teaching and leadership roles at both her *alma mater*. She is Chair of The South Taranaki District Museum Trust, a committee member of Gallery Pātea and a contributing artist. She maintains her passion for education.

Justine Joyce Dreyer, formerly Olckers was born and grew up in Gauteng in the Republic of South Africa. She is a poet, novelist, children's author and a short story writer. She says writing gives her a chance to escape reality and live in her make-believe worlds.

Hannah Oliver says her poem just got into her mind and demanded to come out. It is her first piece of writing since her secondary school days.

OTS. When we asked about who or what OTS was, we didn't get much in the way of clarity, except that two of the initials related to their real name. We are pleased to confirm this it is not a dissident outpost of the Office of Treaty Settlements.

eRiQ Quaadgras was born and raised in Den Haag (The Hague), before moving to Voorburg, Leidschendam, Leiden and now, South Taranaki. Writing has been a passion since childhood and eRiQ says writing is a form of therapy.

The **Paisley Collective** are a band of artists and writers who enjoy collaborative art and writing projects. Their poetry has featured in journals in New Zealand, Australia, the United Kingdom and Canada.

Zoie Parmenter lives and works in the capital in the financial services sector. Her poem was inspired by a summertime break at the Pātea Beach Motor Camp and she half-jokingly says "writing is cheaper than therapy".

Pēwhairangi, Te Kumeroa Ngoingoi was born on 29 December 1921 at Tokomaru Bay, and universally known as Ngoi. She was a leader of Te Hokowhitu-a-Tū Concert Party, which was founded by Tuini Ngāwai, who mentored her. In the 1970s, she tutored Māori at Gisborne Girls High and for the University of Waikato. She was renowned for her spontaneity in writing compositions for various people. Of these songs, 'E ipo', recorded by Prince Tui Teka, and 'Poi e', by Dalvanius Prime and the Pātea Māori Club, are the best known. She also co-invented the Te Ataarangi method of learning Māori with Kātaraina Mataira. Ngoi passed in January 1985.

Panisa Pitigaisorn is based in Bangkok and is a graduate of AUT's celebrated Master of Creative Writing program.

Alice Prendergast says she has a tenuous connection to Waverley through a friend from Waverley who attended Victoria University of Wellington. She says her poem was inspired by her friend's parents' mandarin tree and a love of the art of French painter Paul Gauguin.

Māui Dalvanius Prime (16 January 1948 – 3 October 2002) was a New Zealand entertainer and songwriter. His career spanned 30 years. He mentored many of New Zealand's Māori performers and was a vocal and forthright supporter of Māori culture.

Richard Reeve is an Otago-Dunedin poet. He has published six books of poetry, most recently *Horse and Sheep* (Maungatua Press, 2019) and *Generation Kitchen* (Otago University Press 2015). He lives in Warrington with Octavia and Koshka.

Jessica Pourchi Ruiz is a proud Hondureña and lives with her mother in the capital, Tegucigalpa. She is currently finishing her nursing degree and is looking forward to working in a hospital setting full-time while completing her Master of Nursing at the Hondurean Technical University, beginning in 2023.

P.J. Schaeffer grew up in Taranaki and now lives in Wellington. His familiarity with the area stems from family holidays taken at Waiinu Beach, Waipipi Beach and the campground in Pātea. He has published poems in *Mātātuhi Taranaki* and other journals.

Volodymyr Shevchenko emigrated to the North Shore when his IT consultant father brought his family from Kyiv to Torbay in 2011. His entrée into writing has been helped by collaborations with Trevor Landers.

David Sims is a pseudonym of a seventeen-year veteran as a tanker driver for Fonterra Dairy Co., based at Whareroa, south of Hāwera. He is married, with three children, and lives in Waverley and does indeed drive Fonterra tankers.

The **St. Joseph's Pātea** Poetry Guild has the following members: Marley Ranginui-Hurley, Stephanie Ratahi, Hamuera Wallace-Davis, Raheel Rio, Carlos Hippolite, John Muncaster and Trelise Kingi-Karaitiana.

Michaela Stoneman is and artist and writer who lives in Pātea and owns an art gallery in an old bank building. She also works as the Arts Co-ordinator for the South Taranaki District Council. Check out her website: http://www.mbstoneman.com/

Tanja Tahvanainen hails from the city of Joensuu, in Eastern Finland, near to the border with Russia. She completed her Master's degree at the University of Turku in social work and is a mother and social worker.

Tatiana Thomas hails from the city of Zaporizhzhia in Ukraine, now infamous for its besieged nuclear power plant. She met and married a local Waverley lad and has been resident in Te Aroha since 2011. She works as an accountant on the Hauraki Plains.

Cristina and Mugurel Tudor are two Romanian expats living in Berlin, Mugurel works in IT, Cristina is a photographer with a background in humanities. These definitions have been written in English (which is not their first language), but are rooted in their East-European heritage, with Slavic and Latin influences.

The **Waitōtara School Poetry Posse 2022** is composed of the following members: Aeneas Thomson, Lachlan Mackintosh, Mellissa Burnard, Honor Parsons, Regan Hawken, Mekah Hayward, Coralee McClaren-Coe, Charlie Murphy, Marcus Miller, Temanea Gifkins-Reweti, Harper Ferris, and Noklair Milton.

Evan Wander has fond memories of growing up in Waverley and attending Waverley Primary. Living reasonably close to Dallison Park, his favourite pursuit on a Saturday afternoon was to stand behind the goalposts and collect the rugby balls. His poem is a paean to an old primary school friend.

Richard Woodfield is a sharemilker with no previous experience of having his writing published. He says he has enjoy the experience of being constructively edited and getting guidance and hopes to do more it.

Elvisa Van Der Leden is the Taranaki-Waikato Regional Manager for NZ Forest and Bird, and a former Taranaki Regional Councillor. Her poetry has been published in *Mātātuhi Taranaki: A Bilingual Journal of Literature* Vol.1 (2021), on New Plymouth Phantom Billstickers posters (2018) and she has performed on stage at festivals such as WOMAD (2020).

Richard Venn* is the pseudonym of a white-collar professional who has ties to Whanganui whose real identity has been verified. He enjoys mountain-biking, geocaching and master's swimming.

Veronika Vovchuk trained as a lawyer and is a parliamentary counsel in the House of Deputies, Kyiv, Ukraine. This is her first published poem in English, and it was a collaborative effort based on studying the photo of the old freezing works that originally inspired her co-collaborator.

Michelle Young grew up in Waverley and now is a happy sharemilker who farms a herd of 275 cows in the Manawatū with her husband Robert, and their small children. She says this is her first published poem for 'a very, very, long time' having written for agricultural magazines.

Trevor M Landers grew up in the locality of Kaupokonui-a-Turi and attended school at Sacred Heart, Manaia and Hāwera High School. He has higher degrees from Victoria University of Wellington (MPM, MEd), the University of Canterbury (MA), AUT (MCW) and the University of Melbourne (M-NTCW). He has published poetry volumes nationally and internationally. He is the founding editor of *Mātātuhi Taranaki: A bilingual journal of literature*, believed to be one of the only one of its kind. He is also of Ngāti Airini and Ngāruahine/Taranaki descent. This is his first editorial collaboration with Dr. Vaughan Rapatahana and Ngauru Rawiri.

Vaughan Rapatahana (Te Ātiawa) commutes between homes in Hong Kong, the Philippines, and Aotearoa New Zealand. He is widely published across several genre in both his main languages, te reo Māori and English and his work has been translated into Bahasa Malaysia, Italian, French, Mandarin, Romanian, Spanish. Additionally, he has lived and worked for several years in the Republic of Nauru, PR China, Brunei Darussalam, and the Middle East. He earned a PhD from the University of Auckland with a thesis on Colin Wilson. He has nine collections published variously in Hong Kong SAR; Macau; Philippines; USA; England; France, India, and Aotearoa New Zealand.

Ngauru Rawiri (Ngāti Mutunga, Te Ātiawa, Ngai Tūhoe, Ngāti Pāhauwera) grew up immersed in Te Ao Māori thanks to her linguistical pāpā. Te Waipounamu was her kāinga tupu, however her adult years have been spent in Te Ika a Māui, where she studied health and fitness with Open Polytechnic, and Mātauranga Māori with Te Wānanga o Aotearoa in Ngāmotu. Ngauru is a pouako/teacher of Māori language and cultural studies at Te Pūkenga (The Western Institute of Technology at Taranaki) based in Ngāmotu, she is a researcher for Ngāti Tāwhirikura, and a Health Science student at Massey University. Ngauru has also conducted research for Tamariki Pakari and co-authored a number of publications in various health and medical journals.. She is passionate about the revival of te reo Māori me ōna tikanga, and raising her four bilingual tamariki on the foundations of their tūrangawaewae.

Printed in the USA
CPSIA information can be obtained
at www.ICGtesting.com
LVHW061125120224
771619LV00016B/700